English Olympiad

Class 06

A must have book for all
Olympiads & Talent Search Exams...

by
Srishti Agrawal

BLOOM CAP
Bloom Cap Edu Ventures Pvt. Ltd.

Bloom Cap Edu Ventures Pvt. Ltd.

Administrative & Production Office

'Ramchhaya' 4577/15, Agarwal Road, Darya Ganj, New Delhi -110002
Tele: 011- 47630600, 43518550

ISBN: 978-93-25519-25-1

PRICE: ₹100.00

PO No: TXT-XX-XXXXXXX-X-XX

For further information about the books log on to
www.bloomcap.org

Follow us on

Preface

"Future belongs to those Who prepares for it today"

School Olympiads are National & International level competitions conducted by different Government, Non-Government & Educational Organisations with the purpose of making the children ready to face competitive exams.

The challenging Questions asked in Olympiads motivate them to learn more & more and bring out the best results with improved academic performance. The Awards & Scholarship offered by Olympiads motivate children to aspire & strive for doing better and emerge out to be the best.

English Olympiads

English is one of the most widely spoken languages across the world. In today's era, good command over English is considered as a must have skill. The greatest advantage of studying English is improvement in communication skills along with the growth of personality.

English Olympiads are meant to strengthen students' command over this universal language by improving spellings, grammar, sentence structure and to master student's language skills.

'Bloom English Olympiad Study Book Class 6' is a perfect resource to Study & Practice for Olympiad Exams and other National & State Level Talent Search Exams & Other Competitions.

Some Special Features of Bloom English Olympiad Study Books are;

- Complete coverage of all the aspects of English; Grammar, Reading Comprehension, Writing Skills, Spellings, Vocabulary & Communication Skills.
- Chapterwise Exercises having different types of Objective Questions at par with the Olympiad Level.
- Olympiad Pattern Practice Sets at the end.

This book is prepared by Expert Panel with the utmost care, still if you have any suggestions regarding its improvement then feel free to contact us at olympiads@bloomcap.org. We will try to inculcate your suggestions in the further editions.

Contents

Nouns

1 Mark Questions

Directions (Q. Nos. 1-10) Choose the appropriate nouns from the given options to complete the sentences.

1. He carried a lot of .... to the railway station.
   (a) barrage (b) baggage
   (c) footage (d) garbage

2. The CCTV .... showed the college students stealing the articles from the shop.
   (a) footage (b) loop
   (c) grab (d) studio

3. The headmistrcss joined the investigation ....
   (a) army
   (b) squadron
   (c) bunch
   (d) committee

4. The gold ornaments were hidden in a secret ....
   (a) calamity (b) suit
   (c) cavity (d) copy

5. Osho owned a .... of cars.
   (a) convoy (b) fleet
   (c) troupe (d) swarm

6. The .... clashed with the police violently.
   (a) infants (b) rioters
   (c) toddlers (d) army

7. The French dance .... performed at the city center yesterday.
   (a) troop (b) group
   (c) choir (d) troupe

8. Social media .... allow you to connect with your friends and voice your opinions.
   (a) transforms (b) guidelines
   (c) platforms (d) rules

9. The doctor had to wear the PPE .... before entering the operation theatre.
   (a) clip (b) machine
   (c) kit (d) film

10. The hostel .... allowed the students to go to the nearby market.
    (a) maid (b) barber
    (c) servant (d) warden

Directions (Q. Nos. 11-13) Identify the type of noun for the underlined words in the given sentences.

11. The <u>majority</u> of people were against the new farm laws.
    (a) Collective Noun (b) Material Noun
    (c) Abstract Noun (d) Proper Noun

12. Owning a car was considered a <u>luxury</u> in the 1980s.
    (a) Common Noun (b) Abstract Noun
    (c) Proper Noun (d) Collective Noun

13. George Washington was the first president of the United States.
(a) Abstract Noun (b) Proper Noun
(c) Common Noun (d) Material Noun

Directions (Q. Nos. 14-17) Select the correct Singular/Plural form of the words given in capitals.

14. CHEF
(a) Chefs (b) Chieves
(c) Cheffs (d) Chefes

15. PHENOMENA
(a) Phenomene (b) Phenomenon
(c) Phenoma (d) Phenomine

16. SHEEP
(a) Sheeps (b) Sheepes
(c) Sheep (d) Sheepss

17. CACTI
(a) Cactuss (b) Cactuus
(c) Cact (d) Cactus

Directions (Q. Nos. 18-20) From the given options, find the noun corresponding to the words given in capitals.

18. FAIL
(a) Failed (b) Failness
(c) Fallen (d) Failure

19. OMIT
(a) Omission (b) Omitted
(c) Omitness (d) Omitners

20. EFFICIENT
(a) Efficiency (b) Efficiently
(c) Efficacy (d) Effectiveness

2 Marks Questions

21. Match the following.

List I (Feminine Gender)	List II (Neuter Gender)
A. Mother	1. Sibling
B. Sister	2. Parent
C. Daughter	3. Relative
D. Aunt	4. Child

Codes

	A	B	C	D		A	B	C	D
(a)	3	2	1	4	(b)	1	2	3	4
(c)	4	2	1	3	(d)	2	1	4	3

22. Match the items in List I with their Feminine Gender given in List II.

List I	List II
A. Bull	1. eve
B. Fox	2. cow
C. Tiger	3. vixen
D. Ram	4. tigress

Codes

	A	B	C	D		A	B	C	D
(a)	2	1	4	3	(b)	2	3	4	1
(c)	1	2	3	4	(d)	4	3	2	1

23. On the basis of nouns, which of the following statements is correct?
(a) Witch is the feminine noun of wizard.
(b) Feet is the singular of foot.
(c) Audience, family, team and jewellery are examples of collective noun.
(d) Stars, milk and water are examples of countable noun.

24. On the basis of nouns, which of the following statements is incorrect?
(a) Website, movie, mountain and ocean are examples of common noun.
(b) Air, rain, rice and coffee are examples of uncountable noun.
(c) Ego, childhood, fascination and composer are examples of abstract noun.
(d) Tea, granite, platinum and paint are examples of material noun.

Pronouns

1 Mark Questions

Directions (Q. Nos. 1-6) Choose the correct pronoun from the given options to complete the sentence.

1. The dog barks loudly. .... bark is worse than its bite.
(a) It's (b) His (c) Its (d) Her

2. Is this Jacket .... ?
(a) your (b) her's (c) your's (d) yours

3. Many teams participated in the competition but .... show was the best.
(a) there (b) their (c) theirs (d) here's

4. Manish's parents were in Bengaluru. So were ....
(a) my (b) our (c) mine (d) her's

5. When Sugandha won the lottery. She pinched .... to make sure she wasn't dreaming.
(a) herself (b) himself
(c) her (d) his

6. Dr. Naresh Trehan is .... who I have always admired.
(a) someone (b) no one
(c) everyone (d) anyone

Directions (Q. Nos. 7-11) Identify the type of the underlined pronouns and choose the correct option.

7. He made a friend <u>who</u> was Christian.
(a) Reflexive (b) Possessive
(c) Relative (d) Demonstrative

8. We need a raincoat. Can you give me <u>yours</u>?
(a) Possessive (b) Reflexive
(c) Interrogative (d) Personal

9. They prepared the speech <u>themselves</u>.
(a) Personal (b) Reflexive
(c) Demonstrative (d) Relative

10. Can you bring <u>some</u> masks?
(a) Personal (b) Reflexive
(c) Interrogative (d) Indefinite

11. I don't want <u>that</u> one.
(a) Demonstrative (b) Reflexive
(c) Personal (d) Possessive

Directions (Q. Nos. 12-16) Choose the correct option to replace the words underlined.

12. This is my friend Parul. <u>Parul</u> lives near my house.
(a) He (b) Her
(c) She (d) Him

13. Amit and Rashi are cousins. <u>Amit and Rashi's</u> parents took them to a party.
(a) Them (b) Those
(c) That (d) Their

14. The farmers are protesting at the border. The farmers are planning to stage a tractor rally.
(a) Them (b) Those
(c) They (d) Themselves

15. This pencil is my pencil.
(a) my (b) mine (c) theirs (d) hers

16. Rakul introduced me to Sanvi. Sanvi was Rakul's classmate.
(a) hers (b) him
(c) their (d) her

Directions (Q. Nos. 17-19) Fill in the blanks by choosing the correct pronouns from the given options.

Ankita decided at the beginning of ...**(17)**... session that ...**(18)**... would run for thirty minutes every day. She met a man named Matt one day while she was running. ...**(19)**... told Ankita that he really likes her.

17. (a) their (b) his (c) her (d) her's

18. (a) she (b) they (c) her (d) he

19. (a) Him (b) He (c) She (d) They

2 Marks Questions

20. Replace the underlined words with appropriate pronouns from the options.
Alison and her mother watched the Hurricane on the television. He was named Irma. "Why is everyone talking about the hurricane?" they asked my mother. "The area where the hurricane will hit is populated. They want to get ready for it," said the mother.
(a) It, he, his (b) She, she, his
(c) She, he, her (d) It, she, her

21. On the basis of pronouns, which of the following statements is correct?
(a) 'This' and 'that' are examples of reflexive pronoun.
(b) 'Who', 'which' and 'ourselves' are examples of relative pronoun.
(c) 'Each', 'who', 'anything' and 'why' are examples of indefinite pronoun.
(d) 'Each other' and 'one another' are examples of reciprocal pronoun.

22. Match the following.

List I	List II
A. Shruti and Shivani	1. It
B. Postman	2. I
C. Tiger	3. Them
D. Husband	4. He

Codes

	A	B	C	D		A	B	C	D
(a)	3	2	1	4	(b)	1	2	3	4
(c)	2	1	4	3	(d)	4	2	1	3

Directions (Q. Nos. 23 and 24) Fill in the blanks with correct pronouns.

23. (i) .... really enjoy watching old shows.
(ii) .... are some of the best things on TV.
(i) (a) I (b) Me
(c) My (d) Mine
(ii) (a) Them (b) That
(c) This (d) These

24. (i) These glasses are .... not ....
(ii) .... was present when .... entered the classroom.
(i) (a) mine, yours (b) my, your
(c) my, yours (d) mine, your
(ii) (a) Somebody, her
(b) Nobody, us
(c) Her, somebody
(d) Everybody, I

Verbs

1 Mark Questions

Directions (Q. Nos. 1-5) Choose the verb from the given options.

1. (a) Mercy (b) Junior (c) Merge (d) Pleasant
2. (a) Costume (b) Collage (c) Accost (d) Assumption
3. (a) Enhance (b) Preface (c) Something (d) Spectacular
4. (a) Turbine (b) Garnish (c) Manly (d) Either
5. (a) Production (b) Farther (c) Garner (d) Hostile

Directions (Q. Nos. 6-10) Find the verb/s in the following sentences.

6. Humpty Dumpty sat on a wall.
(a) on (b) sat (c) wall (d) a
7. I am hoping to win the match.
(a) am (b) hoping (c) to (d) Both (a) and (b)
8. We ought to respect our elders.
(a) respect (b) our (c) ought to (d) elders
9. I was working late at night.
(a) was (b) working (c) late (d) Both (a) and (b)
10. Everybody has worked hard today.
(a) Everybody (b) hard (c) has worked (d) today

Directions (Q. Nos. 11-13) Identify the type of the underlined verb in the following sentences.

11. They <u>were</u> cheating from day one.
(a) Transitive (b) Intransitive (c) Helping (d) Modal
12. Roger Federer <u>could</u> play tennis and soccer at the age of eight.
(a) Transitive
(b) Intransitive
(c) Helping
(d) Modal
13. It <u>may</u> be quicker to travel by train.
(a) Modal (b) Transitive (c) Helping (d) Intransitive

Directions (Q. Nos. 14-17) Fill in the blanks by choosing the correct verbs from the options.

14. Prashant quickly .... to living in the new city.
(a) adapted
(b) adopted
(c) adept
(d) halted

15. The teacher asked the student to .... the poem aloud.
(a) red (b) read
(c) reading (d) reads

16. I was anxious while .... for English Olympiad.
(a) reciting (b) sorting
(c) appearing (d) tackling

17. The mechanic .... the computer to remove the faulty component.
(a) assembled (b) dislodged
(c) trimmed (d) disassembled

2 Marks Questions

18. Match the phrasal verbs given in List I with their meanings given in List II.

List I	List II
A. Give up	1. to allow someone to enter
B. Carry on	2. to wait
C. Hold on	3. to stop doing something
D. Let in	4. to continue

Codes

	A	B	C	D
(a)	3	4	1	2
(b)	3	4	2	1
(c)	4	3	2	1
(d)	4	1	3	2

19. Fill in the blanks with suitable verbs from the options.
Mary applied for her passport last month because she will soon be leaving on a trip that she has been .... about for many years. She .... as a receptionist at Ardmore's Travel Agency for ten years.
(a) dreaming, has been working
(b) dreamt, have been worked
(c) dreaming, have been working
(d) dreamt, has been worked

20. Choose the transitive verbs from the following list.

bring arrive enjoy die make happen.

(a) bring, arrive and enjoy
(b) bring, enjoy and make
(c) arrive, die and happen
(d) bring and enjoy

Directions (Q. Nos. 21-23) Which of the following statements have the correct usage of verbs?

21. (a) I went to the party. Did I?
(b) Are we meeting tonight, Parul?
(c) Douglas is been working very long hours lately.
(d) I did enjoyed the outing a lot.

22. (a) Do come and see us some time.
(b) This man can't be a doctor. He look too young.
(c) Did you know that Mozart would play the piano when he was five?
(d) The next train leaving this evening at 1700 hrs.

23. (a) You have always trying to jump over the wall.
(b) He left this bag here and goes outside.
(c) America were a developed nation.
(d) The police is asking about the incident that happened last night.

Chapter 04

Adverbs

1 Mark Questions

Directions (Q. Nos. 1-5) Choose the correct adverb to fill in the blanks.

1. Matt is a regular student. He ……… goes to school.
(a) hardly (b) always
(c) rarely (d) never

2. Kavita is grumpy. She ……… ever smiles.
(a) always (b) surely
(c) hardly (d) mostly

3. The Times of India is published …….. .
(a) weekly (b) lately
(c) monthly (d) daily

4. Shweta spends ……… on purchasing new clothes than on anything else.
(a) most (b) more
(c) sure (d) much

5. Our principal is old ……… to retire.
(a) enough (b) much
(c) quite (d) more

Directions (Q. Nos. 6-10) Identify the adverbs in the given sentences.

6. The PM reacted calmly to the news of the glacier burst in Uttarakhand.
(a) reacted (b) news
(c) burst (d) calmly

7. How did you manage to clear the olympiad?
(a) did (b) clear
(c) how (d) olympiad

8. The actress inaugurated the showroom today.
(a) inaugurated (b) showroom
(c) today (d) the

9. Ronaldo is an extremely talented football player.
(a) talented (b) extremely
(c) football (d) player

10. I looked around but couldn't find my friend.
(a) around (b) find
(c) my (d) looked

Directions (Q.Nos. 11-13) Choose the correct options which the underlined words describe or give more information about.

11. Tapan answered <u>rudely</u> and sat down.
(a) Tapan (b) and
(c) sat (d) answered

12. Covid-19 is <u>highly</u> infectious.
(a) Covid-19 (b) infectious
(c) is (d) All of these

13. Nandita pushed the nozzle forcefully.
(a) nozzle (b) Nandita
(c) the (d) pushed

Directions (Q. Nos. 14-18) Choose the odd one out from the following.

14. (a) Hatred (b) Upright
(c) Tenure (d) Grace

15. (a) Calmly (b) Angrily
(c) Crazily (d) Annoy

16. (a) Weekly (b) Annually
(c) Quietly (d) Daily

17. (a) Here (b) Now
(c) There (d) Everywhere

18. (a) Today (b) Tomorrow
(c) Boldly (d) Then

2 Marks Questions

Directions (Q. Nos. 19-21) Choose the option which gives the correct usage of adverbs in the sentences.

19. (i) The situation at the border is quietly serious.
(ii) The team communicated and played well during the match.

Codes
(a) Only (ii) (b) Only (i)
(c) Both (i) and (ii) (d) None of these

20. (i) Today is much colder than yesterday.
(ii) I came early because I did not want to miss the class.

Codes
(a) Both (i) and (ii)
(b) Only (i)
(c) Only (ii)
(d) None of these

21. (i) An airplane is flying severely over the clouds.
(ii) Phil has been critically injured in a road accident.

Codes
(a) Only (i)
(b) Both (i) and (ii)
(c) Only (ii)
(d) None of the above

Directions (Q. Nos. 22-25) Fill in the blanks with suitable adverbs from the options given below.

22. The snake .... crept toward the boy who was looking .... for the snake.
(a) slow, around
(b) slowly, everywhere
(c) fastly, up
(d) crawling, here and there

23. Ram sang .... to attract attention, but the teacher was watching him ....
(a) louder, moving (b) loud, silent
(c) louser, silently (d) loudly, silently

24. The police discussed the new assignment ...... and ....
(a) briefly, loudly
(b) briefly, secretly
(c) in detail, concealingly
(d) ambiguously, loudly

25. The child was gazing .... at the cake as he wanted to eat it ....
(a) adoringly, completely
(b) adorably, fuel
(c) adoringly, half
(d) adorably, nearly

Adjective

1 Mark Questions

Directions (Q. Nos. 1-6) Choose the adjective form of the following.

1. Grace
   (a) Gracious (b) Graciously
   (c) Gracefulness (d) None of these

2. Skill
   (a) Skilful (b) Skilled
   (c) Skilfully (d) Both (a) and (b)

3. Man
   (a) Manly (b) Manfully
   (c) Manhandle (d) Mane

4. Purity
   (a) Purify (b) Purification
   (c) Pure (d) Purifier

5. Class
   (a) Classified (b) Classy
   (c) Classic (d) All of these

6. Like
   (a) Likely (b) Likelihood
   (c) Likeable (d) Both (a) and (c)

Directions (Q. Nos. 7-11) Fill in the blanks with appropriate adjectives.

7. Ancient, ... coins are exhibited in this museum.
   (a) petty (b) precious
   (c) littlest (d) worthless

8. My dog has blue eyes and .... skin.
   (a) gently (b) softy
   (c) fluff (d) fluffy

9. The .... student was punished by the teacher.
   (a) talkie (b) talked
   (c) talkative (d) polite

10. Dealing in drugs is a .... offence in India.
    (a) puny (b) punishable
    (c) remarkable (d) minor

11. Because of the .... experiences of the past, Suman does not trust people easily.
    (a) bitter (b) bald
    (c) bold (d) combined

Directions (Q. Nos. 12-15) Identify the adjectives in the following sentences.

12. There is a sharp increase in the sale of sanitisers after the Covid-19 pandemic.
    (a) increase (b) sharp
    (c) sanitisers (d) pandemic

13. This jacket is quite comfortable.
    (a) comfortable
    (b) quite
    (c) jacket
    (d) None of the above

14. Whose calculator is this?
(a) whose (b) calculator
(c) is (d) None of these

15. Did you get any information about the vaccination schedule?
(a) Did (b) information
(c) about (d) any

Directions (Q. Nos. 16-18) Replace the underlined words with adjectives from the given options.

16. Kareena loves she pet cat very much.
(a) her (b) its (c) my (d) his

17. Anil goes to school in the bus with he sister.
(a) their (b) our (c) her (d) his

18. You name is Lakshman, isn't it?
(a) Your (b) Our (c) Her (d) Its

Directions (Q. Nos. 19-21) Fill in the blanks with quantifiers from the options given. Hints are given in [ ] after some questions to guide you.

19. In London, in the winter, there's hardly .... sunlight.
(a) some (b) any
(c) many (d) few

20. Could you give me .... your time and your money? [A request – I expect you will say 'yes'.]
(a) each (b) little
(c) enough (d) both

21. Did you buy .... butter? [I expect you will say 'yes', because we talked about it before.]
(a) some (b) any
(c) little (d) less

2 Marks Questions

Directions (Q. Nos. 22 and 23) Identify the error of adjective in the given sentence along with its correction from the given options.

22. There are numeric problems in the farmers' laws.
(a) numeric → numerical
(b) farmers' → farmers
(c) numeric → numerous
(d) farmers' → farmer

23. Many Indians do not have access to portable water.
(a) many → much
(b) portable → potable
(c) many → some
(d) portable → potible

24. Choose the sentences in which adjectives have not been used properly.
A. Everyone knows that a doctor's handwriting is usually illegible.
B. He has a very high temperature.
(a) Only A (b) Only B
(c) Both A and B (d) None of these

25. Which of the following statements use adjectives correctly?
(a) The latter part of the story was more interesting.
(b) The cup has much sugar than I need.
(c) My shirt is best than yours.
(d) What an inedible taste of this apple!

26. Read the statements and choose the correct option.
A. The comparative degree of simple is 'simpler'.
B. The superlative degree of less is 'least'.
C. 'Chilly' is the positive degree of 'chilliest'.
D. 'Some' is an indefinite adjective.
(a) TTFF (b) FTFT (c) TTTF (d) TTTT

Articles

1 Mark Questions

Directions (Q. Nos. 1-10) In each of the questions given below, select the correct option to fill in the blanks (some questions have more than one blank). In all questions, the options are

(a) the
(b) an
(c) a
(d) none

1. Ashok is .... quiet when he's working.
2. .... new student has joined our class today.
3. Wasim usually reaches .... bus stand at about nine o'clock.
4. There is still .... hour for .... train to arrive.
5. Which juice is .... more delicious- apple juice or orange juice?
6. My brother has just bought .... flat.
7. I went to .... bed early last night, but I still feel sleepy.
8. When you enter .... hall, you will see my sofa set.
9. When I wake up in .... morning, I feel fresh.
10. .... work that Yashwant is doing at .... moment sounds boring.

Directions (Q. Nos. 11-14) Choose the sentence with the correct usage of articles.

11. (a) Ritesh went to a party today.
(b) Ritesh went to an party today.
(c) Ritesh went to party a today.
(d) Ritesh went to party an today.
12. (a) Have you heard news about lockdown?
(b) Have you heard the news about an lockdown?
(c) Have you heard news about the lockdown?
(d) Have you heard the news about the lockdown?
13. (a) My uncle is a teacher and lives in Netherlands.
(b) My uncle is the teacher and lives in the Netherlands.
(c) My uncle is a teacher and lives in the Netherlands.
(d) My uncle is teacher and lives in the Netherlands.
14. (a) Is there an university where you live?
(b) Is there a university where you live?
(c) Is there the university where you live?
(d) Is there university where you live?

Directions (Q. Nos. 15-20) Complete the following passage by filling the blanks with the appropriate articles.

France, officially known as ...**(15)**... French Republic, is the largest country in ...**(16)**... European Union by ...**(17)**... area. It has borders with ...**(18)**... English Channel, ...**(19)**... Atlantic Ocean, ...**(20)**... Mediterranean Sea and eight other European countries among them.

15. (a) the (b) a
    (c) an (d) No article

16. (a) a (b) the
    (c) an (d) No article

17. (a) a (b) an
    (c) the (d) No article

18. (a) a (b) an
    (c) the (d) No article

19. (a) the (b) a
    (c) an (d) No article

20. (a) a (b) the
    (c) an (d) No article

2 Marks Questions

21. Match the following.

List I	List II
A. No article	1. X-Ray
B. The	2. Museum
C. A	3. Eiffel Tower
D. An	4. France

Codes

	A	B	C	D		A	B	C	D
(a)	4	3	1	2	(b)	2	3	4	1
(c)	3	1	2	4	(d)	4	3	2	1

Directions (Q. Nos. 22 and 23) Read the statements and choose the correct option.

22. (a) I will go to the airport to pick up my cousin.
    (b) There is no an orange in the fridge.
    (c) A book that you gave me was really boring.
    (d) An house is simply too big for the family.

23. (a) 'The' is not used before Philippines.
    (b) 'An' is used before the word 'honest'.
    (c) 'An' is used before 'unique'.
    (d) No article is used before Japanese.

24. Fill in the blanks with suitable articles.
    Recently, I had .... pleasure of seeing one of Shakespeare's most beloved comedies, 'A Midsummer Night's Dream', performed beautifully at .... Los Angeles Repertory Theatre.
    (a) a, the (b) a, a
    (c) the, a (d) the, The

25. Replace the underlined words with appropriate articles from the option.
    .... butterfly is one of .... most beautiful creatures in the world. They taste with their feet and have .... suction tube for a mouth.
    (a) A, a, the (b) The, a, the
    (c) The, the, a (d) A, the, the

Prepositions

1 Mark Questions

Directions (Q. Nos. 1-5) Fill in the blanks with a preposition by selecting the correct option.

1. All students must reach the school .... 9 AM to be marked present.
(a) on (b) of
(c) before (d) in

2. The Empire State Building in New York was completed .... 1936.
(a) during
(b) on
(c) from
(d) in

3. We all saw Sarita in the stadium .... yesterday.
(a) on (b) (no preposition)
(c) in (d) at

4. All children prepare for attending school .... the end .... June.
(a) at, of (b) on, of
(c) of, in (d) in, for

5. Prakash told him about the accident .... the following day.
(a) at
(b) (no preposition)
(c) in
(d) of

Directions (Q. Nos. 6-10) Choose the sentences with the correct use of prepositions.

6. (a) I will see you on next Friday.
(b) I will see you next on Friday.
(c) I will see you in next Friday.
(d) I will see you next Friday.

7. (a) We're going in two weeks.
(b) We're going on two weeks.
(c) We're going into two weeks.
(d) We're going at two weeks.

8. (a) It showed in the night.
(b) It showed during the night.
(c) It showed between the night.
(d) Both (a) and (b) are correct.

9. (a) I always sit on my best friend in the class.
(b) I always sit next to my best friend in the class.
(c) I always sit under my best friend in the class.
(d) I always sit at my best friend in the class.

10. (a) My boss is terrible on communicating.
(b) My boss is terrible in communicating.
(c) My boss is terrible at communicating.
(d) My boss is terrible with communicating.

Directions (Q. Nos. 11-17) Fill in the blanks with suitable prepositions in the conversation given below.

At the Garage

Customer Have you had a chance ...**(11)**... look ...**(12)**... my car yet?

Mechanic Yes, we've given it a complete examination ...**(13)**... our computerised testing machine.

Customer And what do you think is wrong ...**(14)**... it?

Mechanic That's a bit ...**(15)**... a difficult answer ...**(16)**... give ...**(17)**... a few words.

11. (a) in (b) to (c) (none) (d) of
12. (a) for (b) to (c) at (d) in
13. (a) with (b) at (c) for (d) of
14. (a) to (b) in (c) of (d) with
15. (a) for (b) of (c) in (d) over
16. (a) to (b) under (c) in (d) of
17. (a) at (b) of (c) for (d) in

2 Marks Questions

Directions (Q. Nos. 18 and 19) Fill in the blanks with appropriate prepositions.

My neighbour said she wanted to ask me ...**18(i)**... a favour. Little did I know what was in store for me when I agreed to feet her cat. ...**18(ii)**... my neighbour left on her trip, I walked ...**19(i)**... the street to her house. I looked ...**19(ii)**... the house and couldn't believe what I saw.

18. (i) (a) for (b) to (c) by (d) at
    (ii) (a) above (b) by (c) after (d) when
19. (i) (a) in (b) across (c) through (d) between
    (ii) (a) at (b) from (c) in (d) around

Directions (Q. Nos. 20 and 21) Choose the sentence which does not use prepositions correctly.

20. (a) Once upon a time, there was a beautiful princess.
    (b) I was unable to get out of the appointment.
    (c) Aside from singing, she also plays the piano at the bar.
    (d) The weather will be good this weekend according by Tom.
21. (a) I met him during lunch.
    (b) The Shaker is after the glass.
    (c) The alarm will ring in case of fire.
    (d) Barcelona Football Club's success is behind question.

Directions (Q. Nos. 22-25) Some prepositions in the following sentences are underlined. Replace the ones which have not been used correctly.

22. I complained <u>from</u> the customer service <u>at</u> the issue <u>with</u> my new mixer grinder.
    (a) from (b) with
    (c) at (d) 'from' and 'at'
23. <u>Before</u> I discovered this bar, I used to go straight home <u>after</u> work.
    (a) Before (b) To
    (c) After (d) None of these
24. It was <u>among</u> six in the morning when we made it to bed.
    (a) behind (b) between
    (c) around (d) after
25. The concert will be staged <u>through</u> the month of May.
    (a) throughout (b) on
    (c) below (d) corner

Conjunctions

1 Mark Questions

Directions (Q. Nos. 1-15) Fill in the blanks with suitable coordinating conjunctions from the options given.

1. Hema Malini is a graceful dancer .... people enjoy watching her.
   (a) or (b) nor (c) and (d) but

2. .... the firemen arrived quickly, they could not stop the fire from spreading.
   (a) After (b) Since
   (c) Even if (d) Though

3. .... Pradeep .... Suresh wants to lose, as they are very competitive.
   (a) Both, and (b) Neither, nor
   (c) Not, but (d) Whether, or

4. Several homes burnt down .... a gas pipeline exploded.
   (a) because (b) unless
   (c) until (d) till

5. Ravinder is very good at writing essays, ... Pankaj is good at Science.
   (a) so that (b) both
   (c) whether (d) while

6. Lalit has a very clear idea about what career he wants, ... Mohit is having no idea about his career.
   (a) because (b) unless
   (c) while (d) till

7. Other actors try to imitate Amitabh's style of acting, ... they have not succeeded.
   (a) and (b) yet
   (c) for (d) so

8. Sarita is .... fond of animals .... Rubina is.
   (a) whether, or (b) not, but
   (c) as, as (d) both, and

9. Rashi .... cleared the exam, ... topped the list of successful candidates.
   (a) not only, but also
   (b) either, or
   (c) whether, or
   (d) not, but

10. .... Alok will become an engineer .... a lawyer, he's not sure yet.
    (a) Whether, or (b) Neither, nor
    (c) Both, and (d) Not only, but also

11. Did Lalit phone you in the afternoon .... in the evening?
    (a) but (b) nor
    (c) yet (d) or

12. .... you're here, we will let you in on a secret.
    (a) Unless (b) Nor
    (c) Either (d) Now that

13. He asked .... I needed an umbrella.
(a) if only (b) than
(c) if (d) so that

14. Karun waited .... his sister Manju woke up, as he was not in a hurry to go out.
(a) as (b) unless
(c) but (d) until

15. Srilata told the interviewers that she wanted the job badly, ... she didn't have the required qualifications.
(a) as though
(b) although
(c) till
(d) nor

Directions (Q. Nos. 16 and 17) Choose the sentences with the correct use of conjunctions.

16. (a) We haven't had an outing when the lockdown was announced.
(b) We haven't had an outing for the lockdown was announced.
(c) We haven't had an outing since the lockdown was announced.
(d) We haven't had an outing though the lockdown was announced.

17. (a) Give me something to eat, or I will die out of hunger.
(b) Give me something to eat, else I will die out of hunger.
(c) Give me something to eat, otherwise I will die out of hunger.
(d) All of these are correct

2 Marks Questions

Directions (Q. Nos. 18 and 19) Fill in the blanks with suitable connectors.

It was a very cloudy and windy day. ...**(18)**..., we went sailing on the sea. We took our wind-breaker jackets ...**(19)**... the weather was chilly.

18. (a) Consequently
(b) Even though
(c) In spite of
(d) Nevertheless

19. (a) even though (b) despite
(c) since (d) due to

20. Choose the sentence with incorrect use of conjunction.
(a) As you couldn't see the film, we'll tell you something about it.
(b) She goes to the tennis club because she likes to play tennis.
(c) He reads magazines but he doesn't like to read books.
(d) I am sorry for one is ill and I can't come neither.

Directions (Q. Nos. 21 and 22) Combine the two sentences without changing their meaning.

21. Don't drink any alcohol. You drive carefully.
(a) Don't drink any alcohol even if you drive carefully.
(b) Don't drink any alcohol but you drive carefully.
(c) Don't drink any alcohol and you drive carefully.
(d) Don't drink any alcohol for you drive carefully.

22. They worked hard for the test. They failed the test.
(a) They worked hard for the test, so they failed.
(b) They worked hard for the test, however, they failed.
(c) They worked hard for the test even if they failed.
(d) They worked hard for the test, otherwise they failed.

Sentences

1 Mark Questions

Directions (Q. Nos. 1-3) Choose the sentence from the following which is meaningful and grammatically correct.

1. (a) The actress was alone living.
   (b) Actress the was living alone.
   (c) The actress was living alone.
   (d) Living alone was the actress.

2. (a) The student had an argument with teacher her.
   (b) Student the had argument an with her teacher.
   (c) The student an argument had with teacher her.
   (d) The student had an argument with her teacher.

3. (a) When are you planning to leave?
   (b) Area you planning to leave when?
   (c) When are planning to leave you?
   (d) When you are planning to leave?

Directions (Q. Nos. 4 and 5) Identify the subject in the following sentences.

4. The bartender served the drinks to the guests.
   (a) The bartender
   (b) The bartender served
   (c) the drinks to the guests
   (d) to the guests

5. Rohan, Navin and Nisha decided to come late to school.
   (a) School
   (b) Rohan
   (c) Rohan, Navin
   (d) Rohan, Navin and Nisha

Directions (Q. Nos. 6 and 7) Identify the predicates in the following sentences.

6. She locked the door and went out to play.
   (a) looked the door
   (b) locked the door and
   (c) locked the door and went out to play
   (d) went out to play

7. Kirat and Prabhjot visit the park everyday.
   (a) and Prabhjot visit the park everyday
   (b) visit the park
   (c) visit the
   (d) visit the park everyday

Directions (Q. Nos. 8-11) Read the following sentences and choose their type.

8. The Sun rises in the East.
   (a) Exclamatory (b) Negative
   (c) Optative (d) Assertive

9. May you live long!
(a) Exclamatory (b) Optative
(c) Interrogative (d) Negative

10. Why is everyone looking at me like this?
(a) Declarative (b) Imperative
(c) Interrogative (d) Optative

11. Could you please do me a favour?
(a) Imperative
(b) Exclamatory
(c) Interrogative
(d) Assertive

2 Marks Questions

12. Choose the sentence which is NOT a simple sentence.
(a) My father never works on the weekends.
(b) Mary brushes her teeth twice a day.
(c) They spoke to him in French, but he responded in English.
(d) He drinks coffee every morning.

13. Choose the compound sentence from the following.
(a) She came first, therefore, she got a good seat.
(b) I have no money at the moment
(c) I saw him going to work in the morning when I was going to school.
(d) Because he did not know the route well, he drove slowly.

14. Match the phrases in List I with those in List II to make meaningful sentences.

List I	List II
A. I wish	1. home.
B. Be grateful	2. I could buy that car.
C. In what ways	3. for all that you have.
D. Go back	4. is a spider different from a beetle?

Codes

	A	B	C	D		A	B	C	D
(a)	4	3	2	1	(b)	1	2	3	4
(c)	2	3	4	1	(d)	4	1	2	3

Directions (Q. Nos. 15-18) Transform the given sentences as directed.

15. Change into complex sentence. Without adding the sugar the dish will taste bad.
(a) Add sugar to the dish or it will taste bad
(b) If you do not add sugar to the dish the dish will taste bad.
(c) Whether you add sugar to the dish or not it will taste bad.
(d) Add the sugar to make it taste good.

16. Change into imperative sentence.
Will you, please, open the door?
(a) Open the door.
(b) Open the door, please.
(c) Go and open the door.
(d) Please open the door.

17. Change into assertive sentence.
O that I were young again!
(a) I wish were young again.
(b) Can I be young again?
(c) I would be young agains.
(d) Oh, to be young again.

18. Change into interrogative sentence.
This is not the kind of dress to be worm for a school function.
(a) Isn't this the kind of dress to be worn for a school function?
(b) Is this the kind of dress to be worn for a school function?
(c) What kind of dress to be worn for a school function?
(d) Does this the kind of dress to be worn for a school function?

Tenses

1 Mark Questions

Directions (Q. Nos. 1-9) Select the correct option to fill in the blanks with either the correct Simple Past or Present Perfect Tense of the verb given in brackets after the blank.

1. Yesterday Harish and Sameer .... (go) to the mall.
   (a) were going (b) went
   (c) will go (d) going
2. Aditya .... (certainly / get) good marks in the Hindi test.
   (a) certainly got
   (b) certainly is getting
   (c) certainly getting
   (d) will certainly get
3. My brother, who .... (work) in Kolkata for 10 years, ... (be) now seriously ill.
   (a) working, was
   (b) has been working, is
   (c) will be working, will be
   (d) has work, was
4. I think Sunil .... (start) his journey tomorrow.
   (a) will start
   (b) will started
   (c) will be starting
   (d) have started
5. Our teacher .... (correct) the test papers by Sunday.
   (a) will correct
   (b) will be correcting
   (c) will have corrected
   (d) correcting
6. Varun .... (bring up) by his father because his mother died when he was a baby.
   (a) was bringing up
   (b) has been bring up
   (c) has brought up
   (d) was brought up
7. Savita .... (just/finish) her homework.
   (a) will just finish
   (b) just finishing
   (c) have just finished
   (d) has just finished
8. Sarla's mother .... (stay) in a rented house after her divorce.
   (a) will stays
   (b) will staying
   (c) will be stayed
   (d) has been staying

9. Satish .... (already / travel) to Kashmir twice during the last three years.
   (a) travelled already
   (b) has already travelled
   (c) have already travelled
   (d) already travelling

Directions (Q. Nos. 10-13) Identify the tense used in the following sentences.

10. The Earth rotates on its own axis.
   (a) Present Continuous tense
   (b) Simple Past tense
   (c) Simple Present tense
   (d) Past Continuous tense

11. I have been working at TCS since 2002.
   (a) Present Continuous tense
   (b) Present Perfect tense
   (c) Present Perfect Continuous tense
   (d) Past Perfect tense

12. It was still snowing when I reached Kanpur.
   (a) Present Continuous tense
   (b) Present Perfect tense
   (c) Past Indefinite tense
   (d) Past Continuous tense

13. Naman will have finished his homework when I reach home.
   (a) Present Continuous tense
   (b) Future Continuous tense
   (c) Past Indefinite tense
   (d) Future Perfect tense

Directions (Q. Nos. 14-16) Choose the part that contains an error.

14. My father has left for Brisbane yesterday.
   (a) My father (b) has left
   (c) for Brisbane (d) yesterday

15. The judge asked the culprit if the purse she had stolen contain an i-Phone.
   (a) The judge asked
   (b) the culprit if the purse
   (c) she had stolen
   (d) contain an i-Phone

16. The next online course starts on 15th March. That's what the website say.
   (a) The next online course
   (b) Starts on 15th March
   (c) That's what
   (d) the website say

2 Marks Questions

Directions (Q. Nos. 17 and 18) In the following question a sentence is given with an error. Choose the option that contains the error along with its correction.

17. The judge asked the culprit if the purse she had stolen contain an i-phone.
   (a) The judge asked → The judge asking
   (b) contain an i-phone → contained an i-phone
   (c) she had stolen → she has stolen
   (d) if the purse → of the purse

18. My father has left for Brisbane yesterday.
   (a) has left → had left
   (b) my father → mine father
   (c) for Brisbane → to Brisbane
   (d) yesterday → the previous day

19. Match the following.

List I (Sentences)	List II (Tenses)
A. The Sun sets in the West.	1. Simple Past tense
B. I went to Chanakyapuri yesterday.	2. Present Perfect Continuous tense
C. He has been working on this project since 2008.	3. Present Continuous tense
D. Naveen is riding a bicycle.	4. Simple Present tense

Codes

	A	B	C	D		A	B	C	D
(a)	4	1	3	2	(b)	4	1	2	3
(c)	3	2	4	1	(d)	2	3	4	1

20. Match the following.

List I (Sentences)	List II (Tenses)
A. I have just seen the film.	1. Future Indefinite tense
B. She had wanted to help her brother.	2. Past Continuous tense
C. Pratham was busy in packing yesterday.	3. Past Perfect tense
D. Ritu will take the test tomorrow.	4. Present Perfect tense

Codes

	A	B	C	D
(a)	4	1	2	3
(b)	3	1	2	4
(c)	4	3	2	1
(d)	1	2	3	4

21. Choose the sentence which is NOT in past perfect tense.

(a) She was crying before her father came.

(b) Had the water boiled when you went to the kitchen?

(c) I had never seen such a nice beach before I went to Hawaii.

(d) By the time I returned home, he had already left.

22. Choose the sentence which is in future continuous tense.

(a) The brother will be sleeping in the afternoon.

(b) They haven't gone to the shopping centre.

(c) The Sun was shining everyday that winter.

(d) He had been drinking milk out the carton when Mom walked into the kitchen.

Punctuation

1 Mark Questions

Directions (Q. Nos. 1-5) Choose the correctly punctuated sentences from the following.

1. (a) Amit Neha and Kamna went to see the show organised by Dia Mirza.
   (b) Amit, Neha and kamna went to see the show organised by Dia Mirza.
   (c) Amit, Neha and Kamna went to see the show organised by Dia Mirza.
   (d) Amit, neha and kamna went to see the the show organised by dia mirza.

2. (a) Do you like Dominos or Pizza hut.
   (b) Do you like domino's or pizza hut?
   (c) Do you Like domino's or Pizza Hut?
   (d) Do you like Domino's or Pizza Hut?

3. (a) The farmers organised a tractor Rally on the republic day.
   (b) The Farmers organised a Tractor Rally on the republic Day.
   (c) the farmers organised a tractor rally on the republic day.
   (d) The farmers organised a tractor rally on the Republic Day.

4. (a) I found Sohan's purse on the table, today.
   (b) I found Sohans purse on the table today.
   (c) I found Sohan's purse on the Table today.
   (d) I found Sohan's purse on the table today.

5. (a) What a magnificent shot.
   (b) What a magnificent shot !
   (c) What a magnificent shot?
   (d) What, a magnificent shot !

Directions (Q. Nos. 6-9) Choose the option that shows the correct punctuation and capitalisation for the underlined words.

6. In what ways is the caterpillar different from <u>the Pupa</u>.
   (a) the pupa. (b) the Pupa?
   (c) the pupa, (d) the pupa?

7. On <u>Wednesday, Feb 26 2020</u>-the government announced the vaccination schedule.
   (a) Wednesday, 26th February, 2020,
   (b) wednesday, 26th February, 2020
   (c) Wednesday, 26th February, 2020
   (d) wednesday, 26th February, 2020,

8. "This is the last time I will cook <u>my meal" Pinaki</u> said.
   (a) my meal", Pinaki
   (b) my meal', Pinaki
   (c) my meal, Pinaki
   (d) my meal". Pinaki

9. Jagdish is tired<u>, he"s</u> going home.
   (a) ! he's (b) : he's (c) , he's (d) . He's

2 Marks Questions

Directions (Q. Nos. 10-12) Choose the sentence with incorrect punctuations.

10. (a) "No man can ever lose what he never had", said lzzak Walton.
    (b) Bravo, the United States won the match.
    (c) Namita's brother-in-law has gone to New Zealand.
    (d) Despite all opposition, two more nuclear power stations were built.

11. (a) Whereas we did all the job, they enjoyed themselves.
    (b) You can go to a good university if you work hard, for example, Harvard.
    (c) They didn't like neither Madrid not Texas.
    (d) In particular: tourists should visit London and Manchester.

12. (a) Despite her hard work she doesn't make much money.
    (b) Although studying French seems difficult, it's simpler than you think.
    (c) When you said, you be here, i was arguing with her about this.
    (d) During the war, America tried to stop trading with England.

13. Read the given sentences and state T (TRUE) for the sentence(s) correctly punctuated and F (FALSE) for the sentence(s) incorrectly punctuated.
    (i) My mother-in-law's rants make me furious!
    (ii) We went to the movies, and then we went out to lunch.
    (iii) Swaleha wants the black blue and green dress.
    (iv) Jatin was hurt: he knew she only said to upset him?

    (a) TTTF (b) TTFF
    (c) TFFT (d) FTFT

14. Choose the option with correct punctuation marks.
    (a) Most people have two jobs in order to raise their standards of living; but I don't think it's worth it.
    (b) Most people have two jobs in order to raise their standard of living : But i dont think its worth it!
    (c) Most people have two jobs in order to raise their standard of living; But I don't think its worth it.
    (d) Most people have two jobs in order to raise their standard of living, but I dont think its worth it?

15. Match the following.

List I (Sentence)	List II (Punctuation)
A. Bravo We won the match.	1. (,)
B. Why are you going to town	2. (?)
C. I need water salt noodles and spices.	3. (!)
D. Arent you coming to the party?	4. (')

Codes

	A	B	C	D		A	B	C	D
(a)	3	2	1	4	(b)	1	2	3	4
(c)	2	1	4	3	(d)	4	2	1	3

Active and Passive Voice

1 Mark Questions

Directions (Q. Nos. 1-5) Fill in the blanks with suitable active or passive verb forms from the options given.

1. The injured .... to the hospital in an ambulance.
(a) were taking (b) was taking
(c) were taken (d) have taken

2. Suresh .... reading the book since yesterday.
(a) are (b) has been
(c) have been (d) was

3. My uncle .... writing poems for a while.
(a) has been (b) is
(c) are (d) have been

4. Our Lucknow house .... in 1990 by my father.
(a) built (b) was built
(c) was build (d) has built

5. Shazia and Sharmila .... notes for the examination.
(a) have preparing
(b) been prepared
(c) had preparing
(d) are preparing

Directions (Q. Nos. 6-12) Fill in the blanks with correct words to complete the sentences in active/passive voice.

6. Milk is delivered in the morning.
The milkman .... in the morning.
(a) delivering the milk
(b) delivered the milk
(c) delivers the milk
(d) will deliver the milk

7. The cow is fed by Mohini.
Mohini .... the cow.
(a) feeding (b) is feed
(c) will feed (d) feeds

8. Jagdish answered the question.
The question .... Jagdish.
(a) answered by
(b) was answered by
(c) is answering by
(d) is answered by

9. The mason will build the house in three months.
The house .... the mason in three months.
(a) will be built by (b) is built by
(c) was building by (d) is build by

10. The letter was posted by Varun.
Varun .... the letter.
(a) had posted (b) is posting
(c) will post (d) posted

11. The dolphins had learned many tricks.
Many tricks .... the dolphins.
(a) learned by
(b) is learned by
(c) was learned by
(d) had been learned by

12. My car hit the dog on the road.
The dog on the road .... my car.
(a) hit by
(b) is hitting
(c) was hit by
(d) is hit by

2 Marks Questions

Directions (Q. Nos. 13-17) Choose the correct passive/active voice of the following sentences.

13. The flat tyre was changed by the mechanic.
(a) The flat tyre was being changed by the mechanic.
(b) The flat tyre had been changed by the mechanic.
(c) The mechanic changed the flat tyre.
(d) The mechanic was changing the flat tyre.

14. His grandmother looks after him.
(a) He is looked after by her grandmother.
(b) He has been looked after by his grandmother.
(c) He had been looked after by his grandmother.
(d) He is lo oked after by his grandmother.

15. Did someone tell the students about the trip?
(a) Were the students told about the trip?
(b) Were the students being told about the trip?
(c) Were the students being tell about the trip?
(d) Were the students being told about the trip by someone?

16. By whom this house was built?
(a) Who build this house?
(b) Who was building this house?
(c) Who has built this house?
(d) Who built this house?

17. Someone has cleaned the windows.
(a) The windows have been cleaned by someone.
(b) The windows had been cleaned.
(c) The windows have been cleaned.
(d) The windows has been cleaned by someone.

Directions (Q. Nos. 18 and 19) Choose the option that correctly changes the voice of the given sentence.

18. His father gave Billy a new bicycle.
(a) Billy was given a new bicycle by his father.
(b) A new bicycle is given to Billy by his father.
(c) His father was given a new bicycle by Billy.
(d) A new bicycle was given to his father by Billy.

19. A lot of money was paid to him for the job.
(a) They pay him a lot of money for the job.
(b) He was paid a lot of money for the job.
(c) He paid a lot of money to them for the job.
(d) They paid a lot of money to him for the job.

Direct and Indirect Speech

1 Mark Questions

Directions (Q. Nos. 1-6) Select the correct option to complete the sentence given in indirect/direct speech. In some questions there is more than one blank.

1. "I may lend you some money", promised Milind.
Milind promised that he .... some money.
(a) lend me (b) may lend you
(c) might lend you (d) might lend me

2. The station master said that the Rajdhani Express train would stop there.
The station master said, " The Rajdhani Express train ...."
(a) would stop here (b) would stop there
(c) will stop here (d) will stop there

3. The Science teacher advised Lalita to work hard.
The Science teacher said to Lalita, "............ hard."
(a) You work (b) Work
(c) You can work (d) You like to work

4. "I cannot come", explained Mohini.
Mohini explained that .... come.
(a) she cannot (b) she could not
(c) I cannot not (d) I shall not

5. Mr. Acharya asked the cook whether dinner was ready.
Mr Acharya asked the cook, "............ ready?"
(a) Is dinner
(b) Will dinner be
(c) Dinner is
(d) Was dinner

6. Ramesh said, "I met you yesterday."
Ramesh said that he .... the previous day.
(a) is meeting me
(b) has meet me
(c) had met him
(d) had meet me

Directions (Q. Nos. 7-12) Change the following sentence into indirect/direct speech.

7. Nupur said, "I love the Taj Story Films."
(a) Nupur said that she loves the Taj Story Films.
(b) Nupur said that she loved the Taj Story Films.
(c) Nupur says that she loved the Taj Story Films.
(d) Nupur said that she loved the Taj Story.

8. Kartik said to Kavya, "I'll e-mail you tomorrow."
   (a) Kartik told Kavya that he would email her tomorrow.
   (b) Kartik said to Kavya that he would email her the next day.
   (c) Kartik told Kavya that he would email her the next day.
   (d) Kartik said to Kavya that he would email him the next day.

9. Jay and Vaishali told Kiran that they would do their best in the exam the next day.
   (a) Jay and Vaishali informed to Kiran, "We will do our best in the exam tomorrow."
   (b) Jay and Vaishali told to Kiran, "We will do our best in the exam the next day."
   (c) Jay and Vaishali asked Kiran, "We would do our best in the exam tomorrow."
   (d) Jay and Vaishali said to Kiran, "We will do our best in the exam tomorrow."

10. He said to her. "Please lend me your camera for one day."
   (a) He exclaimed to her to lend him her camera for one day.
   (b) He requested her to lend him your camera for one day.
   (c) He ordered her to lend him her camera for one day.
   (d) He requested her to lend him her camera for one day.

11. They exclaimed with joy that they had won the game.
   (a) They said, "Hurrah! We won the game."
   (b) They said that, "Hurrah! We would win the game."
   (c) They said, "Hurrah! They won the game."
   (d) They told, "Hurrah! They had won the game."

12. The saint wished the women that God might bless me with a child.
   (a) The saint told the woman, "Might God bless you with a child!"
   (b) The saint said to the woman, "May God bless you with a child!"
   (c) The saint said to the woman. "May Cod bless her wuh a child!"
   (d) The saint wished the woman, "May God bless her with a child!"

Directions (Q. Nos. 13-15) Choose the tense that will be used in the direct/indirect speech of the given sentences.

13. Peter said that his mother would celebrate her birthday the following weekend.
   (a) Past Perfect tense
   (b) Simple Present tense
   (c) Simple Past tense
   (d) Simple Future tense

14. Peter said, "I'm playing the piano."
   (a) Past Perfect tense
   (b) Past Perfect Continuous tense
   (c) Past Continuous tense
   (d) Present Perfect tense

15. Arun said that they had not written text messages.
   (a) Present Perfect tense
   (b) Simple Present tense
   (c) Past Perfect Continuous tense
   (d) Present Continuous tense

2 Marks Questions

Directions (Q. Nos. 16 and 17) Choose the option that correctly changes the given sentence into indirect speech.

16. He said, "May you never get peace!"
    A. He cursed that he might never get peace.
    B. He prayed that you might never get peace.
    C. He cursed that she might never get peace.

    Codes
    (a) Only A (b) B and C
    (c) A and C (d) All of these

17. My mother said, "May God bless you!"
    A. My mother cursed that God might bless me.
    B. My mother prayed that God might bless me.
    C. My mother wished that God might bless me.

    Codes
    (a) Only B (b) Only C
    (c) A and B (d) B and C

Directions (Q. Nos. 18 and 19) Choose the sentences which are in indirect speech.

18. A. He told her that he loved her.
    B. The boss told them not to forget.
    C. She admitted breaking the window.
    D. He said, "I will purchase the latest model of i-phone."

    Codes
    (a) A, B and C (b) C and D
    (c) B, C and D (d) Only A

19. A. The interviewer asked me if I spoke French.
    B. Sara asked him if he had finished his work.
    C. Priyali says, "She lives in Delhi.
    D. She advised me not to speak in library.

    Codes
    (a) Only D (b) Only A
    (c) Both B and C (d) A, B and D

20. Read the following sentences and choose which of them are in direct speech.
    A. The old man shouted, "Go to hell!"
    B. He ordered his servant to clean the room.
    C. She said to me that, "please help me!"
    D. Misha said, "Kanishk is checking the computer."

    Codes
    (a) A and D (b) B and D
    (c) Only C (d) A, C and D

Synonyms and Antonyms

1 Mark Questions

Directions (Q. Nos. 1-3) Find a suitable synonym for the underlined word in the following sentences from the given options.

1. The mobile is heavy.
   (a) bulky (b) small
   (c) light (d) sticky
2. Nimrat is terrible at social studies.
   (a) good (b) great
   (c) awful (d) gentle
3. Sulabh gave me an inexpensive gift.
   (a) overpriced (b) expensive
   (c) durable (d) cheap

Directions (Q. Nos. 4-7) In each of the following questions select the option which is the synonym of the given word.

4. Alert
   (a) Hidden (b) Lazy
   (c) Watchful (d) Lively
5. Haughty
   (a) Humble (b) Rich
   (c) Strange (d) Arrogant
6. Frail
   (a) Strong (b) Weak
   (c) Week (d) Careful
7. Alien
   (a) Native (b) Proud
   (c) Foreigner (d) Serious

Directions (Q. Nos. 8-10) Find a suitable antonym for the underlined word in following sentences from the given options.

8. Bill Gates is extremely competent and industrious.
   (a) tireless (b) diligent
   (c) regular (d) lazy
9. Is he fluent in English?
   (a) expressive (b) continuous
   (c) hesitant (d) careless
10. The scarcity of onions led to an increase in its price.
    (a) shortage (b) abundance
    (c) stealing (d) loss

Directions (Q. Nos. 11-14) In each of the following questions, select the option which is the antonym of the given word.

11. Brittle
    (a) Flexible
    (b) Hard
    (c) Breakable
    (d) Weak

12. Generous
(a) Happy
(b) Kind
(c) Stingy
(d) Impartial

13. Obstruct
(a) Hinder (b) Delay (c) Aim (d) Clear

14. Delicious
(a) Edible (b) Inedible
(c) Tasty (d) Bond

2 Marks Questions

15. Match the following.

List I (Words)	List II (Antonyms)
A. Scorn	1. Hostile
B. Increment	2. Disobey
C. Adhere	3. Approve
D. Cordial	4. Reduction

Codes

	A	B	C	D
(a)	4	3	2	1
(b)	3	4	2	1
(c)	3	4	1	2
(d)	2	3	4	1

16. Match the following.

List I (Words)	List II (Synonyms)
A. Feud	1. Disturb
B. Agitate	2. Spat
C. Soothe	3. Sudden
D. Abrupt	4. Calm

Codes

	A	B	C	D
(a)	2	1	3	4
(b)	1	3	2	4
(c)	2	1	4	3
(d)	4	3	2	1

17. Match the following.

List I (Words)	List II (Antonyms)
A. Immense	1. Delight
B. Weary	2. Compliment
C. Insult	3. Energetic
D. Wrath	4. Small

Codes

	A	B	C	D		A	B	C	D
(a)	4	3	2	1	(b)	4	2	3	1
(c)	3	2	4	1	(d)	3	1	2	4

Directions (Q. Nos. 18 and 19) Read the following statements and choose the correct option.

18. (i) The word 'mutual' has a synonym correlative.
(ii) 'Disapproving' is the antonym of 'abusive'.

Codes
(a) Only (i) is true
(b) Both (i) and (ii) are false
(c) Both (i) and (ii) are true
(d) Only (ii) is true

19. (i) 'Closure' and 'Shutdown' are antonyms.
(ii) 'Refined' is the antonym of 'Rustic'.

Codes
(a) Only (ii) is true
(b) Only (i) is true
(c) Both (i) and (ii) are false
(d) Both (i) and (ii) are true

Idioms and Phrases

1 Mark Questions

Directions (Q. Nos. 1-5) Choose the option which gives the correct meaning of the idiom/phrase.

1. Red letter day
   (a) an important day
   (b) a bad day
   (c) a usual day
   (d) a day on which you receive a letter

2. In apple-pie order
   (a) in an unorganised way
   (b) in a quiet way
   (c) in an organised way
   (d) in a frequent manner

3. As fit as a fiddle
   (a) having health issues
   (b) physically fit
   (c) looking like a fiddle
   (d) being temporarily fit

4. At a stone's throw
   (a) very far away
   (b) at a distance of 100 meters
   (c) at an unknown distance
   (d) very close

5. Bring to book
   (a) to mention in a book
   (b) to show in a book
   (c) to gift a book
   (d) to punish

Directions (Q. Nos. 6-10) Choose the correct meaning of the underlined idioms/phrases in the following sentences.

6. Nima was taken to task by her teacher for not completing her homework.
   (a) scolded
   (b) praised
   (c) ignored
   (d) given extra homework

7. The performance by the band was a show-stopper.
   (a) extremely bad (b) very good
   (c) boring (d) repeated

8. Roopali was at her units' end when she was asked by her mother to cook dinner.
   (a) very alert
   (b) very certain
   (c) very confused
   (d) very happy

9. The doctor took a leave as she was feeling under the weather.
   (a) restless (b) lazy
   (c) pain (d) sick

10. Passing the Olympiad is not a piece of cake.
    (a) easy (b) difficult
    (c) good (d) bad

Directions (Q. Nos. 11-15) Complete the following idioms/phrases by filling up the blanks.

11. Eat like a ....
(a) swan (b) pig (c) dog (d) frog

12. A .... republic
(a) potato (b) tomato
(c) banana (d) watermelon

13. .... days
(a) Cat (b) Frog
(c) Turtle (d) dog

14. Shot in the ....
(a) arm (b) leg (c) head (d) bag

15. Cock and .... story
(a) hen (b) bull
(c) wolf (d) parrot

2 Marks Questions

Directions (Q. Nos. 16 and 17) Complete the idioms by matching the items in List I with those in List II.

16.

	List I		List II
A.	Slip of	1.	by the horns
B.	Be tongue	2.	race
C.	Rat	3.	tongue
D.	Take the bull	4.	tied

Codes

	A	B	C	D		A	B	C	D
(a)	3	2	4	1	(b)	3	4	2	1
(c)	3	4	1	2	(d)	4	3	2	1

17.

	List I		List II
A.	Get the	1.	elephant
B.	Hold your	2.	cat
C.	Copy	3.	lion's share
D.	A white	4.	horses

Codes

	A	B	C	D		A	B	C	D
(a)	3	4	2	1	(b)	3	4	1	2
(c)	4	3	2	1	(d)	4	1	3	2

Directions (Q. Nos. 18-20) Read the following statements and choose the correct option.

18. (i) 'In black and white' means in written form.
(ii) To eat humble pie means to admit that you are right.

Codes
(a) Both (i) and (ii) are true
(b) Both (i) and (ii) are false
(c) Only (i) is true
(d) Only (ii) is true

19. (i) More than five thousand cars sold so far. The new model is selling like hot cakes. (Sales very fast)
(ii) We only see the glamor and money in showbiz. But the other side of the coin (rumour) is that only one in hundreds reach there.

Codes
(a) Only (ii) is true
(b) Both (i) and (ii) are true
(c) Both (i) and (ii) are true
(d) Only (i) is true

20. (i) The idiom 'keep an ear to the ground' means to be well informed about events and trends.
(ii) "Hold your tongue (to not speak), son. Be patient", the old men tried to restrain the agitated man.

Codes
(a) Both (i) and (ii) are false
(b) Only (i) is true
(c) Both (i) and (ii) are true
(d) Only (ii) is true

One Word Substitution

1 Mark Questions

Directions (Q. Nos. 1-10) Choose the correct one word substitutions for the following.

1. A woman whose husband is dead.
   (a) Widower (b) Widow
   (c) Spinster (d) Dame

2. One who foretells events.
   (a) Autocrat (b) Democrat
   (c) Astronaut (d) Astrologer

3. One who entertains a guest.
   (a) Spectator (b) Courier
   (c) Host (d) Audience

4. A person who writes beautiful writing.
   (a) Compere (b) Calligrapher
   (c) Astronaut (d) Audience

5. A person who draws maps.
   (a) Cartographer (b) Architect
   (c) Illustrator (d) Presenter

6. A keeper of a museum.
   (a) Traitor (b) Anchor
   (c) Curator (d) Ascetic

7. An examination of a dead body in order to determine the cause of death.
   (a) Suicide (b) Postmortem
   (c) Postdoctoral (d) Alchemy

8. One who works for the welfare of women.
   (a) Egoist (b) Womenist
   (c) Feminist (d) Philanthropist

9. One who holds a post without any salary.
   (a) Volunteer (b) Freeware
   (c) Honourable (d) Honorary

10. One who does not express himself/herself freely.
    (a) Introvert
    (b) Extrovert
    (c) Ambivert
    (d) Cosmopolitan

Directions (Q. Nos. 11-13) Choose the correct meaning of the following one word substitutions.

11. Morgue
    (a) A place where specimen of plants are kept.
    (b) A place where bodies are kept for identification.
    (c) A place where important documents are kept.
    (d) A place where grain kept.

12. Dey
   (a) Nest of a rabbit.
   (b) Nest of a squirrel.
   (c) Nest of an eagle.
   (d) Nest of an owl.

13. Caw
   (a) The sound of cows.
   (b) The sound of a peacock.
   (c) The sound of a hen.
   (d) The sound of a crow.

2 Marks Questions

Directions (Q. Nos. 14-16) Choose the correct one word substitution for underlined part of the sentence.

14. He is someone who can't be believed easily.
   (a) Incredulous (b) Credulous
   (c) Pessimist (d) Bhevolent

15. He can write with both hands.
   (a) Ambiguous (b) Amphibian
   (c) Ambidextrous (d) Alchemist

16. This water is safe to drink.
   (a) Edible (b) Eligible
   (c) Turbid (d) Potable

Direction (Q. Nos. 17 and 18) Choose the correct statement(s).

17. I. Bibliophile : One who loves mankind.
   II. Infanticide : The killing of a new born baby.
   III. Omniscient : One who knows everything.
   IV. Agnostic : One who believes in the existence of God.

   Codes
   (a) Only III (b) Only IV
   (c) Both II and III (d) None of these

18. I. Criminal: a person who has committed a crime.
   II. Murderer: a person who commits murder.
   III. Anarchist : One who promotes revolt against government.
   IV. Pauper : One who has no money.

   Codes
   (a) Both I and III (b) Both II and III
   (c) Only IV (d) All of these

19. Match the following.

List I (One word)		List II (Meaning)
A. Companion	1.	a state formally cooperating with another for a military or other purpose.
B. Ally	2.	a person with whom one works in a profession or business.
C. Colleague	3.	a person or animal with whom one spends a lot of time or with whom one travels.
D. Accomplice	4.	a person who helps another commit a crime.

Codes

	A	B	C	D
(a)	3	1	2	4
(b)	3	4	2	1
(c)	3	1	4	2
(d)	3	2	4	1

Chapter 17

Spelling Test

1 Mark Questions

Directions (Q. Nos. 1-10) Choose the correctly spelt word from the following.

1. (a) Receive (b) Recieve (c) Ricieve (d) Riceive
2. (a) Luggage (b) Lugagge (c) Luggagge (d) Loggage
3. (a) Moisturizerr (b) Moisturriser (c) Moisturiser (d) Mosturiser
4. (a) Allargy (b) Alergy (c) Allergie (d) Allergy
5. (a) Postore (b) Posture (c) Posturre (d) Postuur
6. (a) Cuning (b) Pleasent (c) Carol (d) Suposse
7. (a) Democrasy (b) Summen (c) Patriot (d) Dandruf
8. (a) Parlor (b) Toolkitt (c) Pungant (d) Introvert
9. (a) Butchre (b) Electrician (c) Cosmonautt (d) Nummerical
10. (a) Plateau (b) Remarkabel (c) Receippt (d) Horible

Directions (Q. Nos. 11-15) Choose the misspelt word from the following.

11. (a) Banquet (b) Crechee (c) Constellation (d) Industrious
12. (a) Programme (b) Privilege (c) Humiliation (d) Boycot
13. (a) Ferocious (b) Courageous (c) Engineer (d) Origyn
14. (a) Glacier (b) Dialog (c) Emphasis (d) Jewellery
15. (a) Pout (b) Grouch (c) Spous (d) Couch

Directions (Q. Nos. 16-20) Fill in the blanks with the suitable alphabet provided as the option to make a meaningful word.

16. CO_SEQ_ENCE
(a) N, A (b) N,U
(c) N, N (d) W, U
17. P_UL_RY
(a) A, T (b) O, A
(c) O, T (d) T, O
18. S_NI_I_ER
(a) A, I, S (b) A, T, S
(c) A, S, T (d) T, A, S
19. I_NO_EN_E
(a) G, R, C (b) G, R, S
(c) J, R, C (d) G, R, H
20. DI_IN_ECT_NT
(a) S, F, E (b) E, F, A
(c) E, F, E (d) S, F, A

Directions (Q. Nos. 21-25) Choose the correctly spelt words from the following.

21. (a) Sinserity (b) Proccessing
(c) Trapezium (d) Rombus

22. (a) Petriotism (b) Repubblic
(c) Indigenus (d) Endogenous

23. (a) Creshe (b) Flowerist
(c) Ambigous (d) Conditioning

24. (a) Invantions (b) Invitations
(c) Currancy (d) Occuppancy

25. (a) Creativity (b) Colaboration
(c) Accomodation (d) Nurchuring

2 Marks Questions

Directions (Q. Nos. 26-30) Complete the blanks with the name of the profession described in brackets with its correct spellings from the options given.

26. Neil Armstrong was the first .... (space traveller) to step on the moon.
(a) astronaut (b) asteronaut
(c) astronot (d) aestronaut

27. Kapil's elder sister is the .... (typing letters, keeping records) of a manager in a big company.
(a) sectry (b) secretary
(c) secretery (d) sacretary

28. The passerby took the injured cat to a .... (one who treats animals).
(a) veterinarian (b) veeterinarian
(c) vetrenerian (d) vetterinarian

29. Ravi quarelled with a .... (a lady serving food) in the restaurant because there was a delay in serving him food.
(a) vaiterss (b) waitaress
(c) weiteress (d) waitress

30. The .... (player of music) played the harmonium very badly.
(a) musican (b) musician
(c) musical (d) myusician

Word Pairs and Odd One Out

1 Mark Questions

Directions (Q. Nos. 1-10) Complete the missing word pair in the following.

1. Name and ....
   (a) number (b) address
   (c) age (d) gender
2. Cause and ....
   (a) effect (b) show
   (c) maze (d) affect
3. Give and ....
   (a) grant (b) get
   (c) gape (d) take
4. Huffing and ....
   (a) gruffing
   (b) ranting
   (c) puffing
   (d) showing
5. .... and order
   (a) Flow (b) Law (c) Lo (d) Slow
6. .... and see
   (a) Rate (b) Crate
   (c) Wait (d) Probe
7. High and ....
   (a) fry (b) five
   (c) live (d) dry
8. .... and behold
   (a) Low (b) So
   (c) Slow (d) Lo
9. .... and error
   (a) Prior (b) Try
   (c) Trial (d) Fail
10. .... or less
    (a) For (b) Much
    (c) More (d) Fore

Directions (Q. Nos. 11-20) Choose the odd one out from the following.

11. (a) livid (b) furious
    (c) irate (d) calm
12. (a) preface (b) premises
    (c) blurb (d) ointment
13. (a) prudent (b) bonafide
    (c) solvent (d) malicious
14. (a) disheveled (b) marginalise
    (c) demarcate (d) pushed
15. (a) initially (b) hopefully
    (c) knowingly (d) never
16. (a) bevy (b) troupe
    (c) herd (d) paratrooper

17. (a) Tabloid (b) Periodical
(c) Journal (d) Literature

18. (a) Bovine (b) Ninja
(c) Avian (d) Aquatic

19. (a) Treacherous (b) Bleak
(c) Preachy (d) Inclement

20. (a) Passed (b) may
(c) can (d) ought to

Directions (Q. Nos. 21-25) Fill in the blanks with correct word pairs.

21. They like to get .... on the weekend and explore the countryside.
(a) out and about (b) fish and chips
(c) out and out (d) free and easy

22. They were very worried about him when he was late but he arrived home ....
(a) down and out
(b) bits and pieces
(c) safe and sound
(d) hard and fast

23. The fairytale prince searched the ...... of the kingdom for the beautiful prince.
(a) ins and outs
(b) length and breadth
(c) backwards and forwards
(d) here and there

24. There was no cheating. He won the competition ....
(a) fair and square
(b) forgive and forget
(c) hide and seek
(d) high and mighty

25. After walking in the sun for so long, she was very ....
(a) sixes and sevens
(b) high and low
(c) hot and cold
(d) hot and bothered

2 Marks Questions

Directions (Q. Nos. 26 and 27) Complete the following analogy by choosing the correct option.

26. Heaven : : Heavenly : : Society :
(a) Socially
(b) Social
(c) Solace
(d) Prosocial

27. Create : : Creation : : Significant :
(a) Significance
(b) Signify
(c) Significantly
(d) Signified

28. Which of the following is not a punctuation mark?
(a) (,) (b) (&)
(c) (?) (d) (-)

29. Which of the following is not a dessert?
(a) Ice cream (b) Jam
(c) Samosa (d) Candies

30. Find the odd one out.
(a) A company of actors
(b) a pack of wolves
(c) a clerk of owls
(d) a nye of pheasants

Reading Comprehension

1 Mark Questions

Passage 1

Directions (Q. Nos. 1-5) Read the passage carefully and select the correct options in the questions given.

The Age of Dinosaurs

Today, human beings control Earth. Millions of years ago, before humans existed, dinosaurs ruled Earth. Their fossils have been found all over the world. They ruled Earth for 160 million years. That is much longer than people have been here. Dinosaurs became extinct long before humans existed. Humans and dinosaurs never lived at the same time. Dinosaurs ruled Earth until an unknown catastrophic event made them extinct.

Many scientists believe that a very long time ago, all of the continents were one. As time went by, the continents drifted apart. This explains why dinosaur fossils can be found all over the world. The weather was warmer and more stable than it is today. The temperature would barely rise or fall throughout the year. Therefore, there were no seasons.

Dinosaurs were not alone on the planet. Small mammals and birds existed. There were many reptiles, such as crocodiles and lizards, roaming about. Some fish, sharks, and shellfish were living as well. The Earth had many plants. There was plenty of food to go around and the Earth's creatures maintained a balanced food chain.

No one is sure why the dinosaurs became extinct. There are many theories, but none have been proven.

1. What is this passage mostly about?
   (a) How life would be different if dinosaurs were still alive
   (b) How dinosaurs ruled Earth.
   (c) What dinosaurs ate.
   (d) The age of dinosaurs before they became extinct

2. Which of the following conclusions is supported by information in the passage?
   (a) There was plenty of food to go around during the age of dinosaurs.
   (b) There was a lack of plant and animal diversity during the time of dinosaurs.

(c) Dinosaurs only lived in one section of the earth.
(d) Dinosaurs became extinct when humans came into existence.

3. According to the passage, it is likely that dinosaur fossils are found everywhere because
(a) they lived in many different places
(b) they moved around often
(c) people moved the fossils around
(d) the continents drifted apart

4. As used in the passage, the word 'stable' means ....
(a) uncomfortable
(b) not likely to change
(c) very extreme
(d) threatening

5. In the sentence given below, select the option that best completes it.
Dinosaur fossils have been found all over the earth by humans .... the continents drifted apart after dinosaurs became extinct.
(a) even though
(b) however
(c) because
(d) yet

Passage 2

Directions (Q. Nos. 6-10) Read the passage carefully and select the correct options in the questions given.

Galileo

Galileo Galilei was born in the year 1564 in the town of Pisa, Italy. When he was 20 years old, he was studying in Pisa. His father wanted him to be a doctor, but Galileo was bored with school except for Maths. Because Maths was the one subject where he was doing well, the court mathematician offered to tutor him privately so he could become a qualified mathematician. Galileo's father was disappointed, but he agreed.

Because he needed to earn money, Galileo began experimenting with different things, trying to come up with some sort of invention that he could sell for money. He had a little bit of success with his invention that was like a compass that could be used to measure plots of land. He had already experimented with pendulums, thermometers and magnets.

When he heard that a Dutch inventor had invented something called a spyglass, but was keeping it a secret, Galileo decided to work on one of his own. Within 24 hours, he had invented a telescope that could magnify things to make them appear ten times larger than real life.

One night, he pointed his telescope toward the sky, and made his first of many space observations: the moon was not smooth, like everyone thought. The moon was covered with bumps and craters.

As technology has improved, first Galileo, and then many others, have made improvements on the telescope, the wonderful device that allows us to see from a distance.

6. What do you understand about Galileo from the second sentence of the third paragraph?
(a) Galileo was a slow worker.
(b) Galileo wanted to become famous.
(c) Galileo could measure plots of land with his compass.
(d) Galileo was a great inventor.

7. Which of the following items had Galileo experimented with before inventing the telescope?
   (a) Magnets
   (b) Pendulums
   (c) Thermometers
   (d) All of the above

8. Which one of the following is not true, as per the passage?
   (a) The moon's surface is smooth.
   (b) Galileo's telescope made things appear ten times larger.
   (c) Galileo did well in the Maths subject in school.
   (d) Galileo designed a compass for measuring plots of land.

9. The word 'mathematician' in the first paragraph means ....
   (a) a student of Maths
   (b) an expert in Maths
   (c) a person appointed to a court
   (d) All of the above

10. The word 'magnify' in the third paragraph means ....
   (a) to make something larger
   (b) exaggerate
   (c) to make something appear larger
   (d) make more important

Poem 1

Directions (Q. Nos. 11-15) Read the following poem and answer the questions that follow.

Stopping the Woods on a Snowy Evening.

Whose woods these are I think I know.
His house is in the village though;
He will not see me stopping here
To watch his woods fill up with snow.

My little horse must think it queer
To stop without a farmhouse near
Between the woods and frozen lake
The darkest evening of the year.

He gives his harness bells a shake
To ask if there is some mistake.
The only other sound's the sweep
Of easy wind and downy flake.

The woods are lovely, dark and deep,
But I have promises to keep,
And miles to go before I sleep,
And miles to go before I sleep.

—Robert Frost

11. The woods are covered with
   (a) snow (b) yellow leaves
   (c) sand (d) fallen trees

12. What does the poet mean when he says, "But I have promises to keep"?
   (a) He has to make his life successful.
   (b) He has certain duties which he must discharge.
   (c) He has to follow what he has said to his friends.
   (d) He has to make people happy.

13. The poet is accompanied by
   (a) his friend (b) his donkey
   (c) his horse (d) his cattle

14. The word 'queer' in the poem means
   (a) good (b) helpful
   (c) sticky (d) strange

15. Who gives the harness bells a shake?
   (a) The horse
   (b) The poet
   (c) The horse-rider
   (d) An elephant

Poem 2

Directions (Q. Nos. 16-20) Read the following poem and answer the questions that follow.

Great, wide, beautiful, wonderful World,
With the wonderful water round you curled,
And the wonderful grass upon your breast-
World, you are beautifully drest.
The wonderful air is over me,
And the wonderful wind is shaking the tree,
It walks on the water, and whirls the mills,
And talks to itself on the tops of the hills.
You friendly Earth! how far do you go,
With the wheat-fields that nod and the rivers that flow,
With cities and gardens, and cliffs, and isles,
And people upon you for thousands of miles?
Ah, you are so great, and I am so small,
I tremble to think of you, World, at all;
And yet, when I said my prayers to-day,
A whisper inside me seemed to say,
"You are more than the Earth, though you are such a dot:
You can love and think, and the Earth cannot!"

—**WB Rands**

16. The poet calls the earth
    (a) unfriendly (b) friendly
    (c) proud (d) kind

17. The phrase 'beautifuly drest' in the poem refers to
    (a) wearing costly dresses
    (b) having shiny dresses
    (c) wearing cheap but beautiful dresses
    (d) decorated with nature's beauty

18. Which of the following is the correct meaning of the word 'Cliff'?
    (a) A low area of rock
    (b) A high grassland
    (c) A high area of rock with a very steep side, often at the edge of the sea or a river
    (d) A low grassland

19. Whom does the wind in the poem talk to?
    (a) itself (b) clouds
    (c) passerby (d) birds

20. From the poem we come to know that the poet is .... when he thinks about earth.
    (a) fearless (b) fearful
    (c) proud (d) forgetful

Writing Skills

1 Mark Questions

Directions (Q. Nos. 1-5) A notice is given below with some parts missing, but substituted by numbers 1 to 5. Identify the numbers by selecting the correct options from those given below.

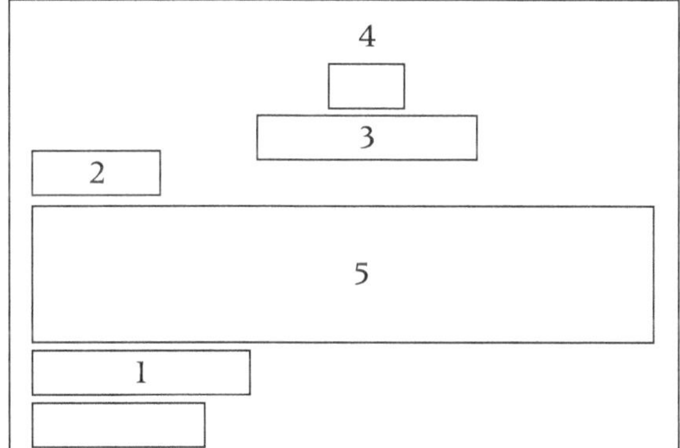

1. The item identified as '1' is
   (a) Name of the organisation
   (b) Name of the issuer of the notice
   (c) Subject of the notice
   (d) Designation of the issuer of the notice

2. The item identified as '2' is
   (a) Subject of the notice
   (b) Designation of the issuer of the notice
   (c) Contents of the notice
   (d) Date of the notice

3. The item identified as '3' is
   (a) Name of the Organisation
   (b) The word 'NOTICE'
   (c) Subject of the notice
   (d) Date of the notice

4. The item identified as '4' is
   (a) Subject of the notice
   (b) Designation of issuer of the notice
   (c) Name of the organisation
   (d) The word 'NOTICE'

5. The item identified as '5' is
   (a) Date of the notice
   (b) Name of the issuer of the notice
   (c) Subject of the notice
   (d) Contents of the notice

Directions (Q. Nos. 6-10) Given below is the format of a formal letter. Choose the correct option to replace the numbers given in the letter.

10
8
6
7
9

6. The item identified as '6' is
   (a) sender's address
   (b) subject of letter
   (c) salutation
   (d) date

7. The item identified as '7' is
   (a) receiver's name
   (b) receiver's address
   (c) body of letter
   (d) salutation

8. The item identified as '8' is
   (a) sender's address
   (b) signature
   (c) salutation
   (d) date

9. The item identified as '9' is
   (a) sender's name and designation
   (b) subscription
   (c) subject of letter
   (d) date

10. The item identified as '10' is
   (a) sender's address
   (b) receiver's address
   (c) salutation
   (d) receiver's name/rank

11. Pallavi writes a message for her mother to inform her that she must get her passport size photo clicked today as her father has to attach them in a form. Choose the correct message which conveys the information appropriately.

(a)

Message
Dear Mother
Get your photo clicked today as father has to attach them on some form.
Pallavi

(b)

Message
2/3/20XX
3:40 PM
Dear Mother
Please get your passport-size photographs clicked today. Father needs them urgently.
Pallavi

(c)

Message
2/3/20XX
3:40 PM
Dear Mother
Please get your passport-sized photos clicked today. Father has to attach them in some form.
Pallavi

(d)

Message
2/3/20XX
3:40 PM
Dear Father
Please get your passport-sized photos clicked today. Mother has to attach them in some form.
Mother

2 Marks Questions

Directions (Q. Nos. 12-16) A message is given below in which different parts are numbered. Identify the parts by choosing the correct option.

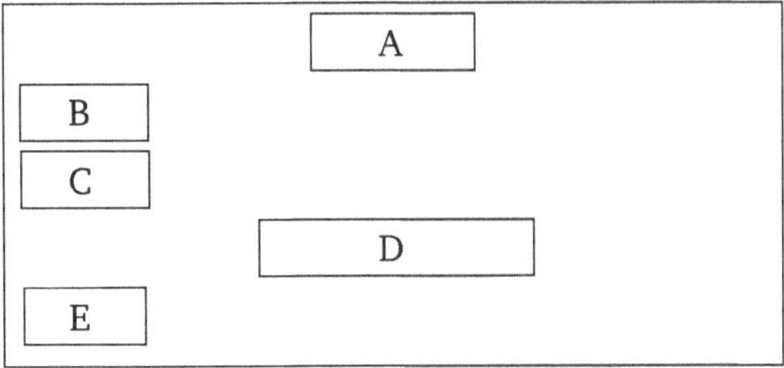

12. Part A is ....
    (a) The word 'Message'
    (b) The Content
    (c) Date of the message
    (d) Name of the person who has written the message

13. Part B is ....
    (a) The word message
    (b) Name of the person who has written the message
    (c) Date of the message
    (d) Time of the message

14. Part E is ....
    (a) Date of the message
    (b) The word Message
    (c) Subject Matter of the message
    (d) Name of the person who has written the message

15. Part D is ....
    (a) The word Message
    (b) Content of the message
    (c) Name of the person who has written the message
    (d) Date

16. Part C is ....
    (a) Salutation
    (b) Date of the message
    (c) Message content
    (d) Time of the message

Directions (Q. Nos. 17-20) Read the conversation and fill the labelled blanks by selecting the appropriate option.

Sheetal : Hello !

Mr. Chatterjee : Hello ! May I speak to Naveen? I am Mr. Chatterjee from his office.

Sheetal : Brother is not at home right now,

Mr. Chatterjee : In that case please give him a message. Please tell him that the meeting fixed for tomorrow has been rescheduled. Ask him to check his official mail account as soon as possible for the details. Please don't forget to inform him.

Sheetal : Don't worry. I will tell her as soon as he returns.

> **Message**
>
> 10th September
>
> 3:25 PM
>
> Naveen
>
> Mr. Chatterjee from **17** called up to say that the **18** fixed for tomorrow has been rescheduled. He wants you to **19** your official mail account as soon as possible for further details.
>
> **20**

17. (a) home (b) conference room (c) office (d) market

18. (a) meeting (b) appointment (c) interview (d) conference

19. (a) send (b) configure (c) see (d) check

20. (a) Mr. Chatterjee
    (b) Sheetal
    (c) Naveen
    (d) Naveen's mother

Chapter 21

Spoken and Written Expression

1 Mark Questions

Directions (Q. Nos. 1-3) Choose the best response for the following.

1. Have you seen my spectacles anywhere?
   (a) You should be knowing where they are.
   (b) How will I know?
   (c) No, I haven't seen them.
   (d) Do you think I have taken them?

2. There is a function at your house. To welcome the guests you will say ....
   (a) Who told you about the function?
   (b) You've come way too early.
   (c) Thank you for coming. Please wait outside for sometime.
   (d) Thank you for coming. Please be seated.

3. Your friend meets with an accident. You decide to write a note for her. How will you start it?
   (a) Hey! What's up?
   (b) Didn't I warn you to drive safely?
   (c) Sorry to hear that you have met with an accident.
   (d) How come you met with an accident?

Directions (Q. Nos. 4-6) Complete the blanks by choosing the correct option.

4. A parent to another parent : Do you know when will the nursery admissions .... ?
   (a) stop (b) end
   (c) start (d) starting

5. Doctor to Patient : You need to follow the social distancing .... and wash your hands ....
   (a) guide, regularly
   (b) guidelines, regular
   (c) guidelining, regularly
   (d) guidelines, regularly

6. Bus conductor to passengers : Please wear your .... and take .... to purchase your tickets.
   (a) gloves, turn (b) masks, turns
   (c) glasses, time (d) masks, time

Directions (Q. Nos. 7-11) Correct the underlined words in the following by replacing them from the ones given in the options.

7. Sumit : Ma'am, <u>can't</u> I come in?
   (a) may (b) can
   (c) would (d) had

8. Rashu : Where are my notes?
   Nisha : I gave them to you. <u>Did I</u>?
   (a) Haven't I? (b) Need I ?
   (c) Didn't I? (d) Didn't we?

9. Neha : Should you like to play with me?
Shreya : Yes. That will be great!
(a) Could (b) Can
(c) May (d) Would

10. Air Hostess to Passengers : Please faster your seat belts.
(a) hasten (b) tie
(c) fasten (d) harden

11. Rakul : Would you mind share your number with me?
Shobhit : Oh Yes, here it is.
(a) mind sharing
(b) minding share
(c) better share
(d) not sharing

Directions (Q. Nos. 12 and 13) Choose the best answer to the following from the options given below.

12. Your neighbour invites you to his house warming party. How will you respond to his invitation?
(a) What will I do at your house?
(b) You should not have invited me.
(c) Thank you for your invitation.
(d) You did not come at my place.

13. Preeti goes to a store to purchase a toy but the shopkeeper doesn't have it. What will the shopkeeper say?
(a) I don't keep such toys.
(b) Why don't you buy this one?
(c) Come some other day.
(d) Sorry, I don't have it.

2 Marks Questions

Direction (Q. Nos. 14-19) Give answer by selecting appropriate option.

14. Rupin : Is this Bhagat Hospital?
Receptionist : ....
(a) Don't you know it?
(b) Yes. How may I help you?
(c) Didn't you check the number before dialing?
(d) Yes. What do you want?

15. Ritika : Please tell me when the online class will start.
School Co-ordinator : ....
(a) You better check on the school's website.
(b) Check the notice board at the school.
(c) It all depends on your teacher.
(d) The classes are likely to start after 10th of this month.

16. Raman : Where can I get the tickets for the cricket match?
Tapan : ....
(a) You know I don't like cricket.
(b) No one knows about it.
(c) You can purchase them online or get them at the Kotla stadium.
(d) You better concentrate on your studies.

17. Naveen : Let's go out for lunch.
Praveen : ....
(a) But I won't pay for it.
(b) Why don't you go with Sukhbir?
(c) Yes, that's a great idea.
(d) Can I also take my cousin with me?

18. Sushmita : My uncle will be taking me to Europe for two weeks.
Kajal : ....
(a) Oh! I will talk to you later.
(b) That's wonderful ! I will mis you a lot.
(c) You should not go with him.
(d) What will happen to your studies?

19. Sagarika : How was your trip, Papa?
Father : ....
(a) Keep to yourself. (b) It was good.
(c) It was awful. (d) Both (b) and (c)

PRACTICE SET 01

1 Mark Questions

1. Select the option which is an antonym of the underlined word in the given sentence.
My sister loves to collect antique furniture.
(a) sturdy (b) weak
(c) modern (d) heavy

Directions (Q. Nos. 2 and 3) Rearrange the part to form a meaningful sentence.

2. The followers
P: praised the Q: the new reforms
R: for brining out S: Prime Minister
(a) PSQR (b) PSRQ
(c) QRSP (d) PQRS

3. The word 'Knife'
P: used to cut
Q: is a general term
R: for any implement
S: pierce, or spread
(a) QRPS (b) PQRS
(c) SQRP (d) QRSP

Directions (Q. Nos. 4 and 5) Choose the odd one out from the following.

4. (a) overseas (b) abroad
(c) upstairs (d) foreign

5. (a) ripped (b) coaster
(c) tinted (d) skinny

6. Choose the correct meaning of the underlined modal verbs in the following sentences.
You can wear what you like, but you must look neat and tidy.
(a) ability
(b) possibility
(c) obligation
(d) prohibition

Directions (Q. Nos. 7 and 8) Choose the correct one word substitution of the following.

7. One who treats skin disease
(a) Dermatologist
(b) Oncologist
(c) Neurologist
(d) Psephologist

8. One who hates women
(a) Pathetic (b) Misogynist
(c) Gourmet (d) Misanthropist

Directions (Q. Nos. 9 and 10) A notice is given below with some parts missing, but substituted by letters A and B. Identify the numbers by selecting the correct options from those given below.

		A
B		

9. The item identified as 'A' is
(a) Subject of the notice
(b) Designation of the issue of the notice
(c) Content of the notice
(d) Name of the organisation

10. The item identified as 'B' is
(a) Name of the organisation
(b) Name of the issuer of the notice
(c) Subject of the notice
(d) Designation of the issuer of the notice

11. Which of the following sentence has the correct usage of articles?
 (a) I came up with an idea while I was taking metro.
 (b) I came up with a idea while I was taking the metro.
 (c) I came up with an idea while I was taking a metro.
 (d) I came up with an idea while I was taking the metro.

12. Choose the sentence with the correct use of conjunctions.
 (a) There are seats outside and some people don't like sitting outdoors.
 (b) There are seats outside but some people don't like sitting outdoors.
 (c) There are seats outside so some people don't like sitting outdoors.
 (d) There are seats outdoors if some people don't like sitting outdoors.

13. Identify the part of speech of the underlined words in the following sentence.
 The BCCI appointed Ravi Shastri as the coach of the Indian Cricket team.
 (a) Conjunction (b) Adverb
 (c) Preposition (d) Adjective

Directions (Q. Nos. 14 and 15) Choose the correct indirect speech of the following sentences.

14. Rupam said, "When I was a child, I wasn't afraid of ghosts."
 (a) Rupam said that when he was a child he wasn't afraid of ghosts.
 (b) Rupam said that when he was a child he hadn't been afraid of ghosts.
 (c) Rupam said that when he was a child he wasn't not afraid of ghosts.
 (d) Rupam said that when he had been a child he wasn't afraid of ghosts.

15. Payal said to Rohan, "I did not go to the movie, did you?"
 (a) Payal told Rohan that she had not gone to the movie and asked him if he had gone.
 (b) Payal asked Rohan if he had gone to the movie.
 (c) Payal told Rohan that she has not gone to the movie and asked him if he has gone.
 (d) Payal said to Rohan that she had gone to the movie and asked him if he had gone.

Directions (Q. Nos. 16 and 17) Fill in the blanks with suitable active or passive verb forms from the options given.

16. The Taj Mahal .... (visit) by millions of people this year.
 (a) will visit
 (b) will be visited
 (c) is visited
 (d) has been visiting

17. Ramesh .... (read, not) the writing of the teacher on the blackboard.
 (a) could not be read
 (b) could not read
 (c) not reading
 (d) will not have read

Directions (Q. Nos. 18 and 19) Choose the synonym of the underlined words in the given sentences.

18. Prisha is an immature girl.
 (a) childish (b) unripe
 (c) unfinished (d) ancient

19. For better health, we must refrain from smoking.
 (a) dissuade (b) desist
 (c) prevent (d) curb

Directions (Q. Nos. 20 and 21) Select the meaning of the underlined idiom in the given sentences.

20. I am waiting for the old man to kick the bucket so that I can get his money.
 (a) to leave (b) to fall ill
 (c) to go in coma (d) to die

21. Some people have the habit of working by fit and starts.
 (a) very seriously (b) excitedly
 (c) consistently (d) irregularly

Directions (Q. Nos. 22 and 23) Fill in the blanks with the correct tense of the verb given in brackets.

22. The train ...... (leave) Nagpur station at 6 PM.
(a) was left (b) had left
(c) had leaved (d) has leaved

23. Polar explorers .... (explore) Antarctica since the beginning of the twentieth century.
(a) will be exploring
(b) has explored
(c) had exploring
(d) have been exploring

24. Which of the following is a possessive pronoun?
(a) It (b) Our
(c) Themselves (d) Mine

25. Which has the correct usage of adverb?
(a) Richly decorated (b) Richly healthy
(c) Greedy rich (d) Greedy power

Directions (Q. Nos. 26 and 27) Choose suitable prepositions to fill the blanks.

26. Are you aware .... the social distancing norms .... the UK, Naina?
(a) about, on (b) of, in
(c) to, on (d) of, at

27. Many protestors came .... to streets .... protest .... the new farm laws.
(a) at, for, with (b) on, to, for
(c) on, to, against (d) into, to, against

28. Which of the words given in the box is/are adjectives?

Polity, Rare, Swindle, Slimy, Wobbly, Pun, Pointed, Live-minded

(a) Polity, Swindle and Slimy
(b) Rare, Slimy, Wobbly and Pointed
(c) Pun, Painted and Woobly
(d) Like-minded, Pointed, Wobbly, Slimy and Rare

Directions (Q. Nos. 29 and 30) Choose the incorrectly spelt word from the following.

29. (a) Ambiguity (b) Honorary
(c) Rampaint (d) Psychology

30. (a) Measals (b) Probability
(c) Neurotic (d) Bonanza

Directions (Q. Nos. 31-35) Fill in the blanks in the following passage by choosing the correct word from the given options.

Ghiyasuddin Tughlaq was the son of a Turkish father ...**(31)**... an Indian mother. He was ...**(32)**... efficient administrator and a capable military commander. He ...**(33)**... several reforms for the welfare of ...**(34)**... subjects. He restored peace and stability ...**(35)**... the Delhi Sultanate.

31. (a) and (b) or (c) but (d) as

32. (a) a (b) an (c) the (d) one

33. (a) introduce (b) introducing
(c) introduced (d) introduces

34. (a) her (b) him (c) he (d) his

35. (a) in (b) on (c) of (d) at

Directions (Q. Nos. 36-40) Read the passage carefully and select the correct options in the questions given.

A thief once hired a room at an inn and stayed there with the intention of stealing some things. The next day when he was thinking of what to do next, he looked out of the window and saw the owner of the inn sitting in the courtyard.

Looking closely, he realised that the owner was wearing an expensive new coat, which the thief decided would look good on himself. To give fruit to his plan, the thief went and sat next to the innkeeper. Striking up a conversation, he got talking about things which were of no interest to either of the two. During the conversation, to the innkeeper's astonishment, he yawned and then howled like a wolf. The innkeeper was curious and asked him as to why did he do that? The thief said he had no control over his yawning and if he yawned three times, he actually turned into a wolf. He begged the innkeeper not to leave him, as he was frightened. Moreover, with that he yawned again and let out another howl. The innkeeper turned pale and got up to go, but the thief caught hold of his coast and begged him to stay. Even as he pleaded, he yawned again. The terrified innkeeper wriggled out of the coat to which the thief was tightly holding on, ran into the inn, and locked himself in. The thief calmly put on the coat and walked away.

36. What did the thief want to do?
(a) Stay at the inn without paying.
(b) Steal the innkeeper's coat.
(c) Change into a wolf.
(d) Talk to the innkeeper.

37. The thief turning into a wolf was ....
(a) an actual fact
(b) in the innkeeper's imagination
(c) a story for tourists
(d) a story made up by the thief

38. What will be a suitable title of the story?
(a) A scared innkeeper
(b) The thief who became a wolf
(c) The intelligent thief
(d) The tempting coat

39. Which of the following is the synonym of the word 'curious' in the passage?
(a) Interested (b) Strange
(c) Surprising (d) Disinterested

40. Which word in the passage means the same as 'plan'?
(a) Requirement (b) Interest
(c) Things (d) Intention

2 Marks Questions

41. Choose the sentences which have NOT been punctuated properly.
A. Nakul, Parth and I went to a party at the Maurya Sheraton, New Delhi.
B. Mrs Roy keeps an open house on Saturday evening.
C. "Come and join me for a drink." Nishant said.
D. Why are you wasting your time.
Codes
(a) A and B (b) C and D
(c) B and C (d) A, B and C

42. On the basis of prepositions, choose the correct option.
(a) 'Under', 'and', 'but' and 'since' are examples of preposition.
(b) 'Beside' and 'Besides' can be used interchangeably.
(c) 'With', 'despite', 'towards' and 'throughout' are examples of preposition.
(d) 'Which', 'how', 'what' and 'over' are examples of preposition.

43. Match the phrasal verbs given in List I with their meanings given in List II.

	List I		List II
A.	Round up	1.	explode
B.	Look for	2.	to arrest
C.	Drop in	3.	to search
D.	Blow up	4.	to pay a short visit

Codes

	A	B	C	D		A	B	C	D
(a)	2	3	1	4	(b)	4	3	2	1
(c)	3	2	4	1	(d)	2	3	4	1

44. Read the statements and choose the correct option.
A. 'May' is used to express a wish or prayer.
B. 'Parliament' is a collective noun.
C. 'Solemn' means serious.
D. 'Abundant' and 'Scarce' are synonyms.
(a) FFFT (b) TTTT
(c) TFTF (d) TTTF

45. Which of the following sentences are grammatically correct and meaningful?

A. My father is a honourable man who doesn't take bribes.

B. How could you a greenhorn like Dilip for the Job?

C. If you can't say something nice, don't say anything at all.

D. What is a difference between 'knife' and 'dagger'?

Codes

(a) A and D (b) B and C
(c) Only C (d) Only B

46. Match the words in List I with those in List II to make word pairs.

	List I		List II
A.	Tech	1.	Ended
B.	Open	2.	Sawy
C.	Rat	3.	Throat
D.	Cut	4.	Race

Codes

	A	B	C	D
(a)	2	1	4	3
(b)	3	2	1	4
(c)	4	1	3	2
(d)	4	2	3	1

47. Which of the following sentence has the incorrect usage of the word 'Cast'.

A. The director throw a party for the coast after the huge success of the film.

B. Votes have been cast in Delhi today.

C. The actor belonged to a low cast.

D. The moon cast as while light everywhere.

Codes

(a) Only A (b) Only B
(c) B and C (d) Only C

48. Read the following statements and choose the correct option.

A. 'I've' is the short form of I has.

B. 'The' is used after the name of famous buildings.

C. 'Hard' and 'Hardly' are adverbs.

D. 'Fetal' is the incorrect spelling of 'Fatal'.

(a) FFFT (b) FTTF (c) TTFF (d) TTTT

49. Match the phrases in List I to those given in List II to make meaningful sentences.

	List I		List II
A.	An ultrasound scan	1.	and started shouting angrily
B.	Is the government doing	2.	against the poor
C.	He entered the room	3.	revealed tissue damage
D.	No one should discriminate	4.	something to stop the second wave of Covid-19?

Codes

	A	B	C	D		A	B	C	D
(a)	3	4	2	1	(b)	1	2	3	4
(c)	2	3	4	1	(d)	3	4	1	2

50. Choose the option that gives the correct part of speech for the underlined words in the sentences.

A. Rupali can climb the stairs in 10 seconds.

B. I was late for work today.

C. Though he is very intelligent, he could not clear the interview.

D. Adversity teaches man many things.

(a) Noun, Conjunction, Verb, Noun
(b) Verb, Preposition, Adverb, Noun
(c) Verb, Preposition, Conjunction, Adverb
(d) Verb, Preposition, Conjunction, Noun

PRACTICE SET 02

1 Mark Questions

Directions (Q. Nos. 1 and 2) Choose the odd one out from the following.

1. (a) Partly (b) Heavenly (c) Socially (d) Partially

2. (a) Pretend (b) Motionless (c) British (d) Depressed

Directions (Q. Nos. 3-5) Choose the incorrectly spelt words from the following.

3. (a) Gratitude (b) Carnivorous (c) Jaundise (d) Parliamentary

4. (a) Received (b) Portrayal (c) Paratrooper (d) Custodien

5. Choose the correctly spelled word from the following.
   (a) Profesional (b) Rastaurant (c) Guarantee (d) Oppurtunity

Directions (Q. Nos. 6-9) Fill in the blanks by choosing the correct word from the options.

6. He came up with a .... idea to reduce air pollution.
   (a) nobel (b) novel (c) noble (d) nimble

7. All children love chocolate ice cream, and Naina is .... exception.
   (a) no (b) not (c) not an (d) now

8. The constant .... from his boss made Ranjani's life at work intolerable.
   (a) apprehension (b) criticism (c) summation (d) retention

9. Would you like .... cheese?
   (a) any (b) one (c) some (d) few

Directions (Q. Nos. 10-12) Rearrange the following parts to make a meaningful sentence.

10. Mr. Raj has
    P: to be disturbed
    Q: that he is not
    R: instructions
    S: given strict
    (a) SRPQ (b) PQRS (c) RQSP (d) SRQP

11. You're our party leader,
    P: how can
    Q: of other people's beliefs?
    R: so intolerant
    S: you be
    (a) PSRQ (b) PQRS (c) QRSP (d) SRQP

12. English coaching institutes,
    P: promise to make you
    Q: which have
    R: mushroomed on every street,
    S: fluent in six months
    (a) QSRP (b) QRPS (c) RSQP (d) PQRS

Directions (Q. Nos. 13-15) Select the correctly punctuated sentences from the following.

13. (a) What is the meaning of 'be in it for the long haul'.
    (b) What is the meaning of 'be in it for the long haul'?
    (c) what is the meaning of 'be in it for the long haul'?
    (d) What is the meaning of 'be in it for the long haul?

14. (a) After the French revolution had taken place, many other European countries were concerned about civil unrest.
    (b) After the French revolution had taken place, many other European countries were concerned about civil unrest.

(c) After the French Revolution had taken place, many other European countries were concerned about civil unrest.

(d) After the French Revolution had taken place, many other European countries were concerned about Civil Unrest.

15. (a) A single red guava has over 200 mg of vitamin C in 100 grams.

(b) A single red guava has over 200 MG of vitamin C is 100 Grams.

(c) A single red guava has over 200 MG of vitamin C in 100 grams.

(d) A single red guava has over 200 mg of Vitamin C in 100 grams.

Directions (Q. Nos. 16 and 17) Choose the correct meaning of the underlined idioms in the given sentences.

16. Natasha broke down in the middle of her speech.

(a) could not proceed
(b) fell down
(c) became angry
(d) cried

17. The speaker gave a bird's eye view of the political conditions of his area.

(a) a detailed presentation
(b) a biased view
(c) a general view
(d) a personal view

Directions (Q. Nos. 18 and 19) Replace the underlined articles in the sentence with the correct ones.

18. Mildy is a everyday shampoo which can be used for daily cleaning and conditioning of the hair.

(a) the, a (b) an, an
(c) an, a (d) an, No article

19. 'Open' is a autobiography by Andre Agassi, the retired tennis player, who later became the tennis coach.

(a) an, a, a
(b) an, No article, No article
(c) the, a, a
(d) an, a, an

Directions (Q. Nos. 20 and 21) Change the following sentences into indirect speech.

20. The waiter said, "Do you want a table near the window?"

(a) The waiter asked if I want a table near the window.

(b) The waiter asked if I wanted a table near the window.

(c) The waiter said if I want a table near the window.

(d) The waiter said if I wanted a table near the window.

21. The guard said, "You must not enter the area as it has not been sanitised."

(a) The guard warned us not enter the area as it had been sanitised.

(b) The guard warned us not entering the area as it had not been sanitised.

(c) The guard warned us not to enter the area as it had not been sanitised.

(d) The guard warns us not to enter the area as it had not been sanitised.

22. Complete the following word pair by choosing the correct option.

...... and cheese

(a) Milk (b) Salt (c) Pepper (d) Chalk

Directions (Q. Nos. 23 and 24) Which of the following sentences has the correct use of tenses.

23. (a) When I am a boy, I walked a mile to school every day.

(b) When I were a boy, I walked a mile to school every day.

(c) When I was a boy, I walked a mile to school every day.

(d) When I was a boy, I walks a mile to school every day.

24. (a) I'm having a party this weekend. Would you liked to come?

(b) I'm having a party this weekend. Would you like to come?

(c) I'm having a party this weekend. Would you likes to come?

(d) I'm have a party this weekend. Would you like to come?

Directions (Q. Nos. 25 and 26) Choose the correct passive voice of the following sentences.

25. People consider that she is honest.
   (a) It is considered by the people that she is honest.
   (b) It was considered by the people that she is honest.
   (c) It has been considered that she is honest.
   (d) It is considered that she is honest.

26. Could you pass the sugar?
   (a) Could the sugar been passed?
   (b) Could the sugar be passed by anyone?
   (c) Could the sugar be past?
   (d) Could the sugar be passed?

27. Which of the following sentence has incorrect use of adverbs?
   (a) Nutan opened the door quietly.
   (b) She spoke angrily.
   (c) We usually spend our holidays in Mussorie.
   (d) The builders are working slowly really.

28. Choose the correct synonym of the following.
   Scorn
   (a) Concise (b) Contempt
   (c) Fierce (d) Calm

Directions (Q. Nos. 29 and 30) Choose the correct antonym of the underlined word in the following sentences.

29. There are no permanent <u>adversaries</u> in politics.
   (a) associates (b) allies
   (c) collaborators (d) partners

30. There is no trace of <u>vanity</u> in the actress behaviour.
   (a) humility (b) selflessness
   (c) modesty (d) dignity

Directions (Q. Nos. 31-35) Read the passage carefully and answer the questions that follow.

Once a man saw three masons along with some labourers who were constructing a temple. He observed the masons for some days and found that though the three of them were doing the same kind of work, there was a marked difference in their approach to their job.

He saw that the first mason reported for his work late, did his work half-heartedly and sluggishly enjoyed longer rest intervals, frequently checked the time on his wrist-watch and left the work before time. The second mason was very punctual in arriving and leaving, and did his work methodically and conscientiously.

The third mason, however, would come before time, took few intervals and often worked overtime.

The man naturally got curious and wanted to know the three mason's outlook towards their work. He asked them what they were doing. The first mason tapped his protruding belly with his hand and said, "I am earning fuel for this belly." The second said, "I am constructing a building." The third looked at the stately building and said "I am building the house of God."

31. The writer is trying to tell the readers that ....
   (a) all work and no play is healthy.
   (b) all play and no work is healthy.
   (c) enjoy doing work with commitment.
   (d) All of the above

32. The first mason's approach to work was that of ....
   (a) earning his livelihood.
   (b) passing the time.
   (c) earning only money.
   (d) wasting time.

33. The third mason approached his work with ....
   (a) eagerness
   (b) skill
   (c) duty
   (d) dedication

34. The phrase, 'work is worship' can be associated with ....
   (a) the first mason
   (b) the second mason
   (c) the third mason
   (d) all the three masons

35. Which word from the passage means the opposite of 'vigorously'?
(a) conscientiously (paragraph 2)
(b) sluggishly (paragraph 2)
(c) half-heartedly (paragraph 2)
(d) stately (paragraph 3)

Directions (Q. Nos. 36-40) Read the following passage and fill in the blanks by choosing the appropriate words from the given options.

It was Valentine's Day 14th February. The year ...**(36)**... 1876. But what happened ...**(37)**... that day in a U.S. patent office surely didn't sow the seeds of love.

Hours within each other representative of two men arrived at ...**(38)**... patent office. The representative of Scottish-born ...**(39)**... Alexander Graham Bell handed in a patent application to the patent office for an apparatus that ...**(40)**... vocal sounds through electricity lines, or, in other words, a telephone.

36. (a) is (b) were
(c) was (d) has

37. (a) in (b) at
(c) of (d) on

38. (a) the (b) a
(c) an (d) a/an

39. (a) inventors (b) invent
(c) inventing (d) inventor

40. (a) transmits (b) transmit
(c) transmitting (d) transmitted

2 Marks Questions

41. Select the grammatically correct and meaningful sentences from the following.
A. Using more and more chemical hair products may bring negative results to your hair.
B. Brushing with a wrong type of brush may harm the hair seriously.
C. What are you doing to improves your quality of life?
D. The quick brown fox jumped into the lazy dog.

Codes
(a) A and D (b) B, C and D
(c) A and B (d) A, B and C

42. Unjumble the jumbled words given in List I and match them with their correct forms given in List II.

	List I		List II
A.	SSSRET	1.	BOWLER
B.	HSARH	2.	STRESS
C.	ERBWLO	3.	DAMAGE
D.	AEMDAG	4.	HARSH

Codes

	A	B	C	D
(a)	2	4	3	1
(b)	3	2	1	4
(c)	4	3	2	1
(d)	2	4	1	3

43. Match the adjectives in List I with nouns given in List II to make meaningful combinations.

	List I		List II
A.	Rash	1.	Disaster
B.	Heated	2.	Call
C.	Close	3.	Driving
D.	Utter	4.	Argument

Codes

	A	B	C	D		A	B	C	D
(a)	3	4	1	2	(b)	3	4	2	1
(c)	1	2	3	4	(d)	4	2	3	1

44. Read the following statements and choose the correct option.
A. 'The' should not be used before Netherlands.
B. That place had a terrible weather yesterday. Here 'fessible' is an adjective.

(a) Only A is true
(b) Both A and B are false
(c) Only B is true
(d) Both A and B are true

45. Which of the words given in the box are nouns, adjectives and conjunctions?

but, on, hardly, sober, equipment upon, hinder abroad, plantation, because

(a) but, because, sober
(b) but, on, because, sober, plantation, equipment
(c) on, hardly, abroad, hinder, upon
(d) equipment, sober, but, plantation, because

46. Match the phrases in List I with those in List II to make meaningful sentences.

	List I		List II
A.	Using such	1.	win if you never begin.
B.	You will never	2.	products can lead to dandruff.
C.	Radar equipment	3.	know exactly what they're getting.
D.	People want to	4.	is used to detect enemy aircraft.

Codes

	A	B	C	D		A	B	C	D
(a)	2	1	3	4	(b)	2	1	4	3
(c)	4	3	2	1	(d)	3	1	4	2

47. Read the following statements and choose the correct statement as True (T) and incorrect statements as False (F).

A. 'Equipment' is an uncountable noun.
B. 'Formulae' is the plural of 'Formula'.
C. 'stingy' is an adverb.
D. 'An' is not used before 'uncle'

(a) TTFF (b) TFFF
(c) FFTT (d) FFFT

48. Choose the correct synonym/antonym pairs from the following.

A : attractive-ugly
B : stingy-miser
C : fat-plump
D : nocturnal-diurnal
E : chaotic : calm
F : simple-complex

(a) C, B and E
(b) A, D and E
(c) A, B, C and D
(d) A, C, D, E and F

49. Choose the sentences with the correct use of words
'stole', 'steal', 'stale' and 'steel'.

A. One should not eat stale food.
B. Niharika stole a pair of jeans from the godown.
C. They have an annual production of two million tons of steal.
D. Steel is an alloy of iron and carbon.

Codes

(a) A, B and C
(b) A and B
(c) A, B and D
(d) B and D

50. Read the following statement and choose the correct option.

A. Notice is an informal means of communication.
B. It is not necessary to mention your address in a formal letter.

Codes

(a) Both A and B are false
(b) Both A and B are true
(c) Only A is true
(d) Only B is true

ANSWERS

Chapter 1 Nouns

1. (b)	**2.** (a)	**3.** (d)	**4.** (c)	**5.** (b)	**6.** (b)	**7.** (d)	**8.** (c)	**9.** (c)	**10.** (d)
11. (a)	**12.** (b)	**13.** (c)	**14.** (a)	**15.** (b)	**16.** (c)	**17.** (d)	**18.** (d)	**19.** (a)	**20.** (a)
21. (d)	**22.** (b)	**23.** (a)	**24.** (c)						

Chapter 2 Pronouns

1. (c)	**2.** (d)	**3.** (b)	**4.** (c)	**5.** (a)	**6.** (a)	**7.** (c)	**8.** (a)	**9.** (b)	**10.** (d)
11. (a)	**12.** (c)	**13.** (d)	**14.** (c)	**15.** (b)	**16.** (d)	**17.** (c)	**18.** (a)	**19.** (b)	**20.** (d)
21. (d)	**22.** (a)	**23.** (i) (a), (ii) (d)	**24.** (i) (a), (ii) (d)						

Chapter 3 Verbs

1. (c)	**2.** (c)	**3.** (a)	**4.** (b)	**5.** (c)	**6.** (b)	**7.** (d)	**8.** (c)	**9.** (d)	**10.** (c)
11. (c)	**12.** (d)	**13.** (a)	**14.** (a)	**15.** (b)	**16.** (c)	**17.** (d)	**18.** (b)	**19.** (a)	**20.** (b)
21. (b)	**22.** (a)	**23.** (d)							

Chapter 4 Adverbs

1. (b)	**2.** (c)	**3.** (d)	**4.** (b)	**5.** (a)	**6.** (d)	**7.** (c)	**8.** (c)	**9.** (b)	**10.** (a)
11. (d)	**12.** (b)	**13.** (d)	**14.** (b)	**15.** (d)	**16.** (c)	**17.** (b)	**18.** (c)	**19.** (a)	**20.** (a)
21. (c)	**22.** (b)	**23.** (d)	**24.** (b)	**25.** (a)					

Chapter 5 Adjective

1. (a)	**2.** (d)	**3.** (a)	**4.** (c)	**5.** (d)	**6.** (d)	**7.** (b)	**8.** (d)	**9.** (c)	**10.** (b)
11. (a)	**12.** (b)	**13.** (a)	**14.** (a)	**15.** (d)	**16.** (a)	**17.** (d)	**18.** (a)	**19** (b)	**20.** (d)
21. (a)	**22.** (c)	**23.** (b)	**24.** (d)	**25.** (a)	**26.** (d)				

Chapter 6 Articles

1. (d)	**2.** (c)	**3.** (a)	**4.** (b,a)	**5.** (d)	**6.** (c)	**7.** (d)	**8.** (a)	**9.** (a)	**10.** (a,a)
11. (a)	**12.** (d)	**13.** (c)	**14.** (b)	**15.** (a)	**16.** (b)	**17.** (d)	**18.** (c)	**19** (a)	**20.** (b)
21. (d)	**22.** (a)	**23.** (b)	**24.** (d)	**25.** (c)					

Chapter 7 : Prepositions

1. (c)	**2.** (d)	**3.** (b)	**4.** (a)	**5.** (b)	**6.** (d)	**7.** (a)	**8.** (d)	**9.** (b)	**10.** (c)
11. (b)	**12.** (c)	**13.** (a)	**14.** (d)	**15.** (b)	**16.** (a)	**17.** (d)	**18.** (i) (a) (ii) (c)	**19.** (i) (b) (ii) (d)	**20.** (d)
21. (d)	**22.** (d)	**23.** (d)	**24.** (c)	**25.** (a)					

Chapter 8 Conjunctions

1. (c) 2. (d) 3. (b) 4. (a) 5. (d) 6. (c) 7. (b) 8. (c) 9. (a) 10. (a)
11. (d) 12. (d) 13. (c) 14. (d) 15. (b) 16. (c) 17. (d) 18. (d) 19. (c) 20. (d)
21. (c) 22. (b)

Chapter 9 Sentence

1. (c) 2. (d) 3. (a) 4. (a) 5. (d) 6. (c) 7. (d) 8. (d) 9. (b) 10. (c)
11. (a) 12. (c) 13. (a) 14. (c) 15. (b) 16. (a) 17. (a) 18. (b)

Chapter 10 Tenses

1. (b) 2. (d) 3. (b) 4. (a) 5. (c) 6. (d) 7. (d) 8. (d) 9. (b) 10. (c)
11. (c) 12. (d) 13. (d) 14. (b) 15. (d) 16. (d) 17. (b) 18. (a) 19. (b) 20. (c)
21. (a) 22. (a)

Chapter 11 Punctuation

1. (c) 2. (d) 3. (d) 4. (d) 5. (b) 6. (d) 7. (a) 8. (a) 9. (d) 10. (b)
11. (d) 12. (c) 13. (b) 14. (a) 15. (a)

Chapter 12 Active and Passive Voice

1. (c) 2. (b) 3. (a) 4. (b) 5. (d) 6. (c) 7. (d) 8. (b) 9. (a) 10. (d)
11. (d) 12. (c) 13. (c) 14. (d) 15. (a) 16. (d) 17. (c) 18. (a) 19. (d)

Chapter 13 Direct and Indirect Speech

1. (d) 2. (c) 3. (b) 4. (b) 5. (a) 6. (c) 7. (b) 8. (c) 9. (d) 10. (d)
11. (a) 12. (b) 13. (d) 14. (c) 15. (a) 16. (c) 17. (d) 18. (a) 19. (d) 20. (a)

Chapter 14 Synonyms and Antonyms

1. (a) 2. (c) 3. (d) 4. (c) 5. (d) 6. (b) 7. (c) 8. (d) 9. (c) 10. (b)
11. (a) 12. (c) 13. (d) 14. (b) 15. (b) 16. (c) 17. (a) 18. (a) 19. (a)

Chapter 15 Idioms and Phrases

1. (a) 2. (c) 3. (b) 4. (d) 5. (d) 6. (a) 7. (b) 8. (c) 9. (d) 10. (a)
11. (b) 12. (c) 13. (d) 14. (a) 15. (b) 16. (b) 17. (a) 18. (c) 19. (d) 20. (c)

Chapter 16 One Word Substitution

1. (b) 2. (d) 3. (c) 4. (b) 5. (a) 6. (c) 7. (b) 8. (c) 9. (d) 10. (a)
11. (b) 12. (b) 13. (d) 14. (a) 15. (c) 16. (d) 17. (c) 18. (d) 19. (a)

Chapter 17 Spelling Test

1. (a)	**2.** (a)	**3.** (c)	**4.** (d)	**5.** (b)	**6.** (c)	**7.** (c)	**8.** (d)	**9.** (b)	**10.** (a)
11. (b)	**12.** (d)	**13.** (d)	**14.** (b)	**15.** (c)	**16.** (b)	**17.** (c)	**18.** (b)	**19.** (a)	**20.** (d)
21. (c)	**22.** (d)	**23.** (d)	**24.** (b)	**25.** (a)	**26.** (a)	**27.** (b)	**28.** (a)	**29.** (d)	**30.** (b)

Chapter 18 Word Pairs and Odd One Put

1. (b)	**2.** (a)	**3.** (d)	**4.** (c)	**5.** (b)	**6.** (c)	**7.** (d)	**8.** (d)	**9.** (c)	**10.** (c)
11. (d)	**12.** (b)	**13.** (c)	**14.** (a)	**15.** (d)	**16.** (d)	**17.** (a)	**18.** (b)	**19.** (c)	**20.** (a)
21. (a)	**22.** (c)	**23.** (b)	**24.** (a)	**25.** (d)	**26.** (b)	**27.** (a)	**28.** (b)	**29.** (c)	**30.** (c)

Chapter 19 Reading Comprehension

1. (d)	**2.** (a)	**3.** (d)	**4.** (b)	**5.** (c)	**6.** (d)	**7.** (d)	**8.** (a)	**9.** (b)	**10.** (c)
11. (a)	**12.** (b)	**13.** (c)	**14.** (d)	**15.** (a)	**16.** (b)	**17.** (d)	**18.** (c)	**19.** (a)	**20.** (b)

Chapter 20 Writing Skills

1. (b)	**2.** (d)	**3.** (c)	**4.** (c)	**5.** (d)	**6.** (b)	**7.** (d)	**8.** (d)	**9.** (a)	**10.** (a)
11. (c)	**12.** (a)	**13.** (c)	**14.** (d)	**15.** (b)	**16.** (d)	**17.** (c)	**18.** (a)	**19.** (d)	**20.** (b)

Chapter 21 Spoken and Written Expression

1. (c)	**2.** (d)	**3.** (c)	**4.** (c)	**5.** (d)	**6.** (b)	**7.** (a)	**8.** (c)	**9.** (d)	**10.** (c)
11. (a)	**12.** (c)	**13.** (d)	**14.** (b)	**15.** (d)	**16.** (c)	**17.** (c)	**18.** (b)	**19.** (d)	

Practice Set-1

1. (c)	**2.** (b)	**3.** (a)	**4.** (c)	**5.** (b)	**6.** (c)	**7.** (a)	**8.** (b)	**9.** (d)	**10.** (b)
11. (d)	**12.** (b)	**13.** (c)	**14.** (a)	**15.** (a)	**16.** (b)	**17.** (b)	**18.** (a)	**19.** (b)	**20.** (d)
21. (d)	**22.** (b)	**23.** (d)	**24.** (d)	**25.** (a)	**26.** (b)	**27.** (c)	**28.** (d)	**29.** (c)	**30.** (a)
31. (a)	**32.** (b)	**33.** (c)	**34.** (d)	**35.** (a)	**36.** (b)	**37.** (d)	**38.** (c)	**39.** (a)	**40.** (d)
41. (b)	**42.** (c)	**43.** (d)	**44.** (d)	**45.** (c)	**46.** (a)	**47.** (d)	**48.** (b)	**49.** (d)	**50.** (d)

Practice Set-2

1. (b)	**2.** (a)	**3.** (c)	**4.** (d)	**5.** (c)	**6.** (b)	**7.** (a)	**8.** (b)	**9.** (c)	**10.** (d)
11. (a)	**12.** (b)	**13.** (b)	**14.** (c)	**15.** (a)	**16.** (d)	**17.** (c)	**18.** (d)	**19.** (a)	**20.** (b)
21. (c)	**22.** (d)	**23.** (c)	**24.** (b)	**25.** (d)	**26.** (d)	**27.** (d)	**28.** (b)	**29.** (b)	**30.** (a)
31. (c)	**32.** (a)	**33.** (d)	**34.** (c)	**35.** (b)	**36.** (c)	**37.** (d)	**38.** (a)	**39.** (d)	**40.** (a)
41. (c)	**42.** (d)	**43.** (b)	**44.** (c)	**45.** (d)	**46.** (b)	**47.** (a)	**48.** (d)	**49.** (c)	**50.** (a)

www.ingramcontent.com/pod-product-compliance
Lightning Source LLC
LaVergne TN
LVHW080106160726
843469LV00047B/1916

9789325519251